HMH SCIENCE DIMENSIONS™

Volume 1

Grade 5
Units 1–4

This Write-In Book belongs to

_____

Teacher/Room

_____

Houghton Mifflin Harcourt™

Consulting Authors

Michael A. DiSpezio
Global Educator
North Falmouth, Massachusetts

Marjorie Frank
Science Writer and Content-Area
  Reading Specialist
Brooklyn, New York

Michael R. Heithaus, PhD
Dean, College of Arts, Sciences &
  Education
Professor, Department of Biological
  Sciences
Florida International University
Miami, Florida

Cary Sneider, PhD
Associate Research Professor
Portland State University
Portland, Oregon

Printed in the U.S.A.
ISBN 978-1-328-90542-0

8 9 10 0877 25 24 23 22 21 20
4500815468   C D E F G

Program Advisors

Paul D. Asimow, PhD
Eleanor and John R. McMillan Professor of Geology and Geochemistry
California Institute of Technology
Pasadena, California

Eileen Cashman, PhD
Professor
Humboldt State University
Arcata, California

Mark B. Moldwin, PhD
Professor of Space Sciences and Engineering
University of Michigan
Ann Arbor, Michigan

Kelly Y. Neiles, PhD
Assistant Professor of Chemistry
St. Mary's College of Maryland
St. Mary's City, Maryland

Sten Odenwald, PhD
Astronomer
NASA Goddard Spaceflight Center
Greenbelt, Maryland

Bruce W. Schafer
Director of K–12 STEM Collaborations, retired
Oregon University System
Portland, Oregon

Barry A. Van Deman
President and CEO
Museum of Life and Science
Durham, North Carolina

Kim Withers, PhD
Assistant Professor
Texas A&M University-Corpus Christi
Corpus Christi, Texas

Adam D. Woods, PhD
Professor
California State University, Fullerton
Fullerton, California

Classroom Reviewers

Michelle Barnett
Lichen K–8 School
Citrus Heights, California

Brandi Bazarnik
Skycrest Elementary
Citrus Heights, California

Kristin Wojes-Broetzmann
Saint Anthony Parish School
Menomonee Falls, Wisconsin

Andrea Brown
District Science and STEAM Curriculum TOSA
Hacienda La Puente Unified School District
Hacienda Heights, California

Denice Gayner
Earl LeGette Elementary
Fair Oaks, California

Emily Giles
Elementary Curriculum Consultant
Kenton County School District
Ft. Wright, Kentucky

Crystal Hintzman
Director of Curriculum, Instruction and Assessment
School District of Superior
Superior, Wisconsin

Roya Hosseini
Junction Avenue K–8 School
Livermore, California

Cynthia Alexander Kirk
Classroom Teacher, Learning Specialist
West Creek Academy
Valencia, California

Marie LaCross
Fair Oaks Ranch Community School
Santa Clarita, California

Emily Miller
Science Specialist
Madison Metropolitan School District
Madison, Wisconsin

Monica Murray, EdD
Principal
Bassett Unified School District
La Puente, California

Wendy Savaske
Director of Instructional Services
School District of Holmen
Holmen, Wisconsin

Tina Topoleski
District Science Supervisor
Jackson School District
Jackson, New Jersey

You are a scientist!

You are naturally curious.

Have you wondered . . .

- is ice still water?
- if you could float in midair?
- how you can talk to your friend on a cell phone?
- if plants can grow without soil?

_____

_____

_____

Write in some other things you wonder about.

HMH SCIENCE DIMENSIONS™

will SPARK your curiosity

AND prepare you for

✓ tomorrow
✓ next year
✓ college
or career
✓ life

Where do you see yourself in 20 years?

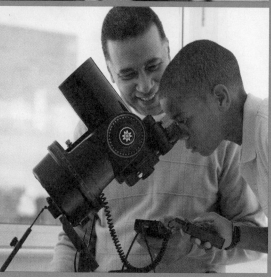

Write in
or draw
another career
you'd like.

Be a scientist.

Work like real scientists work.

Plan

Investiga

Have Fun

Be an engineer.
Solve problems like engineers do.

Design

Solve Problems

Share Solutions

Explain your world.

Start by asking questions.

Think Critically

Make a Claim

Gather Evidence

There's more than one way to the answer. What's YOURS?

Work in Teams

Develop Explanations

Support Your Conclusions

UNIT 1 Engineering and Technology

Engineering and Technology 1

Energy and Matter in Organisms

Systems in Space

Safety in the Lab

Doing science is a lot of fun. But, a science lab can be a dangerous place. Falls, cuts, and burns can happen easily. **Know the safety rules and listen to your teacher.**

☐ **Think ahead.** Study the investigation steps so you know what to expect. If you have any questions, ask your teacher. Be sure you understand all caution statements and safety reminders.

☐ **Be neat and clean.** Keep your work area clean. If you have long hair, pull it back so it doesn't get in the way. Roll or push up long sleeves to keep them away from your activity.

☐ **Oops!** If you spill or break something, or get cut, tell your teacher right away.

☐ **Watch your eyes.** Wear safety goggles anytime you are directed to do so. If you get anything in your eyes, tell your teacher right away.

☐ **Yuck!** Never eat or drink anything during a science activity.

☐ **Don't get shocked.** Be careful if an electric appliance is used. Be sure that electric cords are in a safe place where you can't trip over them. Never use the cord to pull a plug from an outlet.

☐ **Keep it clean.** Always clean up when you have finished. Put everything away and wipe your work area. Wash your hands.

☐ **Play it safe.** Always know where to find safety equipment, such as fire extinguishers. Know how to use the safety equipment around you.

Safety in the Field

Lots of science research happens outdoors. It's fun to explore the wild! But, you need to be careful. The weather, the land, and the living things can surprise you.

- [ ] **Think ahead.** Study the investigation steps so you know what to expect. If you have any questions, ask your teacher. Be sure you understand all caution statements and safety reminders.

- [ ] **Dress right.** Wear appropriate clothes and shoes for the outdoors. Cover up and wear sunscreen and sunglasses for sun safety.

- [ ] **Clean up the area.** Follow your teacher's instructions for when and how to throw away waste.

- [ ] **Oops!** Tell your teacher right away if you break something or get hurt.

- [ ] **Watch your eyes.** Wear safety goggles when directed to do so. If you get anything in your eyes, tell your teacher right away.

- [ ] **Yuck!** Never taste anything outdoors.

- [ ] **Stay with your group.** Work in the area as directed by your teacher. Stay on marked trails.

- [ ] **"Wilderness" doesn't mean go wild.** Never engage in horseplay, games, or pranks.

- [ ] **Always walk.** No running!

- [ ] **Play it safe.** Know where safety equipment can be found and how to use it. Know how to get help.

- [ ] **Clean up.** Wash your hands with soap and water when you come back indoors.

Safety Symbols

To highlight important safety concerns, the following symbols are used in a Hands-On Activity. Remember that no matter what safety symbols you see, all safety rules should be followed at all times.

Dress Code

- Wear safety goggles as directed.
- If anything gets into your eye, tell your teacher immediately
- Do not wear contact lenses in the lab.
- Wear appropriate protective gloves as directed.
- Tie back long hair, secure loose clothing, and remove loose jewelry.

Glassware and Sharp Object Safety

- Do not use chipped or cracked glassware.
- Notify your teacher immediately if a piece of glass breaks.
- Use extreme care when handling all sharp and pointed instruments.
- Do not cut an object while holding the object in your hands.
- Cut objects on a suitable surface, always in a direction away from your body.

Electrical Safety

- Do not use equipment with frayed electrical cords or loose plugs.
- Do not use electrical equipment near water or when clothing or hands are wet.
- Hold the plug when you plug in or unplug equipment.

Chemical Safety

- If a chemical gets on your skin, on your clothing, or in your eyes, rinse it immediately, and tell your teacher.
- Do not clean up spilled chemicals unless your teacher directs you to do so.
- Keep your hands away from your face while you are working on any activity.

Heating and Fire Safety

- Know your school's evacuation-fire routes.
- Never leave a hot plate unattended while it is turned on or while it is cooling.
- Allow equipment to cool before storing it.

Plant and Animal Safety

- Do not eat any part of a plant.
- Do not pick any wild plant unless your teacher instructs you to do so.
- Treat animals carefully and respectfully.
- Wash your hands throughly after handling any plant or animal.

Cleanup

- Clean all work surfaces and protective equipment as directed by your teacher.
- Wash your hands throughly before you leave the lab or after any activity.

Safety Quiz

Circle the letter of the BEST answer.

1. Before starting an activity, you should
   a. try an experiment of your own.
   b. open all containers and packages.
   c. read all directions and make sure you understand them.
   d. handle all the equipment to become familiar with it.

2. At the end of any activity, you should
   a. wash your hands thoroughly before leaving the lab.
   b. cover your face with your hands.
   c. put on your safety goggles.
   d. leave the materials where they are.

3. If you get hurt or injured in any way, you should
   a. tell your teacher immediately.
   b. find bandages or a first aid kit.
   c. go to your principal's office.
   d. get help after you finish the activity.

4. If your equipment is chipped or broken, you should
   a. use it only for solid materials.
   b. give it to your teacher for recycling or disposal.
   c. put it back.
   d. increase the damage so that it is obvious.

5. If you have unused liquids after finishing an activity, you should
   a. pour them down a sink or drain.
   b. mix them all together in a bucket.
   c. put them back into their original containers.
   d. dispose of them as directed by your teacher.

6. When working with materials that might fly into the air and hurt someone's eye, you should wear
   a. goggles.
   b. an apron.
   c. gloves.
   d. a hat.

7. If you get something in your eye, you should
   a. wash your hands immediately.
   b. put the lid back on the container.
   c. wait to see if your eye becomes irritated.
   d. tell your teacher right away.

Engineering and Technology

Explore Online

Unit Project: Dropping Off, Picking Up
How can the front of the school be redesigned to improve the way students are dropped off and picked up? Ask your teacher for more project information.

Prototype gear made by a 3D printer

At a Glance

Vocabulary Game: Concentration

Materials
• 1 set of word cards

Setup
• Mix up the cards.
• Place the cards face down on a table in even rows. Each card should not touch another card.

Directions
1. Take turns to play.

2. Choose two cards. Turn the cards face up.
   • If the cards match, keep the pair and take another turn.
   • If the cards do not match, turn them back over.

3. The game is over when all cards have been matched. The players count their pairs. The player with the most pairs wins.

erosion

The process of moving sediment from one place to another

Unit Vocabulary

 **brainstorming:** Collecting as many ideas as you can, however good you think they are.

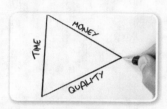 **constraint:** A real world limit on the solution you are designing, for example, safety, time, money, or materials.

 **criteria:** The desirable features of a solution.

 **deforestation:** The process of cutting down trees to plant crops.

 **erosion:** The process of moving sediment from one place to another.

 **tradeoff:** The process of giving up one quality or feature of a design to gain a different quality or feature.

How Are Science and Math Used in Engineering?

On a clear night in the city, it can be hard to see the stars. Streetlights, headlights, and lights in buildings can dim starlight. Earth's atmosphere also has a blurring effect on our view of stars from Earth. That's one reason the Hubble Space Telescope was sent into space in 1990. It orbits above Earth and gives us a clearer view of space.

By the end of this lesson . . .
you'll be able to describe how science and math are used in engineering.

Can You Solve It?

 Explore Online

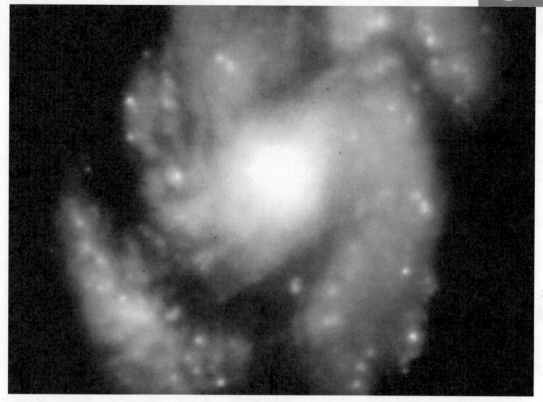

Almost right after launch, a problem was found with the Hubble Space Telescope. It was not able to take clear pictures and see different parts of space as well as it was built to do. NASA was faced with a big engineering problem: How do you fix a telescope in orbit? Luckily, they figured out a solution.

1. What do you think was wrong with the telescope? How do you think NASA fixed the Hubble telescope?

_____

_____

_____

_____

_____

 EVIDENCE NOTEBOOK Look for this icon to help you gather evidence to answer the questions above.

What Is Engineering?

What Is Technology and What Is Not?

Look around you. What are some of the things that you see? A chair? A door? a car? All of these things are products of engineering, which is the practical use of science and math to solve problems to meet needs and wants. Engineered objects can be simple. You can change a stick to a tool by breaking off a twig and using it to dig a hole. Engineered objects can also be complex such as a communication satellite that orbits Earth.

What are some other things that are products of engineering?

2. Look over each of the objects below. Decide which ones are examples of technology and which are not examples of technology. Draw lines to match each object to the proper box: Engineered or Not Engineered.

calculator

wooden chair

| **Engineered** | truck | **Not Engineered** |

plant

computer

insect

3. What evidence did you use to decide how to sort the items?

_____

_____

_____

_____

 HANDS-ON Apply What You Know

In Touch with Technology

4. With a partner, take turns describing what today's breakfast or trip to school would have been like if there were no technology. Together, write down one true statement about technology that your descriptions show. Be prepared to share it.

Factory Engineering

How can we define technology? A good way to do this is to say that technology is the products and processes designed to solve a problem or meet a need. Engineering makes technology.

Some examples of technology that engineers designed are smartphones and cars. Technology is even used to make the food you eat. Look at the images below to see technology used in a bakery. For each step in the process, think about how an engineer designed the machines.

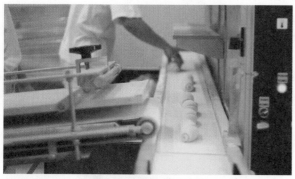

STEP 1 A machine rolls bread dough into cylinders and then drops them on a conveyor belt.

STEP 2 The dough is kneaded and shaped by a machine.

STEP 3 The conveyor belt carries the dough into ovens.

STEP 4 The baked loaves cool on the conveyor belt.

5. Look at the objects listed. Choose each object that is an example of something an engineer helped design.
    a. tree
    b. lamp
    c. fire alarm
    d. T-shirt
    e. printer

Technology Everywhere

When you think of technology, what do you visualize? A computer? A space telescope? You might think of technology as complex machines that are very technical. But technology is anything made by people that meets a need.

We live in an engineered world. As you walk through a park, there are bicycles and park benches. As you walk into a mall, there are lights shining, escalators moving, and automatic doors opening. Nearly everything around us is technology.

Look around your classroom. Most of the objects you see are examples of technology. A pencil, for example, is technology. It helps you communicate by writing. It is not as complex as a smartphone that allows you to communicate by texting, but both meet the need of communication.

The student in this photo is using scissors, a kind of technology, to cut paper.

6. Where are you least likely to see technology? Why?

_____

_____

_____

_____

_____

Classroom Technology

7. Match the descriptions to the technology in the classroom and add labels.

a. _____
An engineer helped to design the case and keys, and a computer engineer helped to make it solve complex math problems.

b. _____
A chemical engineer improved the quality of the glass, while a mechanical engineer designed the frame so it is easy to use.

c. _____
A mechanical engineer helped make it by designing machines to print, cut the paper, and bind it together.

d. _____
A mechanical engineer helped build the machines used to cut and stitch the cloth together.

8. What two things do all the objects have in common as examples of technology?

_____

_____

Tech Knowledge

Now that you have learned about technology and how we define it, research online one piece of technology. Write down the needs or wants that it meets. Take note of at least two sources that you used to get information.

Now pair up with another student and test each other. Ask each other what the piece of technology is and why it is technology. Also ask how it meets wants or needs.

9. What is your piece of technology? What are some of the wants and needs that it meets?

_____

_____

_____

_____

EVIDENCE NOTEBOOK The Hubble telescope had many different scientists and engineers working on it to make it work well. When it did not work as expected, it showed that something needed to be fixed. Think about the situation that the scientists and engineers faced and answer the following question in your Evidence Notebook. What need or want did the Hubble project have?

Putting It Together

Technology is all around us and in almost everything that we see. From our homes to schools, there are traffic lights and ovens and other types of technology. Humans have been designing solutions to meet wants and needs for a long, long time.

10. What is the purpose of technology?

_____

_____

_____

Tip

Combine details from different sources to clarify or strengthen your main ideas. Reading and Writing in Science.

How Does Engineering Use Science?

Engineering Vision

Scientists discover new things about the world and universe around us. Engineers use these scientific discoveries to help design and make new technology. Ideas can build on one another over time to produce totally new solutions.

Look over each image. Think about how new scientific discoveries helped engineers design each item.

Early studies of optics, the science of light interacting with matter, helped people engineer antique spectacles.

Polymer chemists discovered lighter, tougher plastics. Engineers used them to design lightweight plastic frames and thinner, lighter lenses.

Scientific discoveries with water-absorbing plastics led to soft contact lenses. People often prefer them for sports and activities.

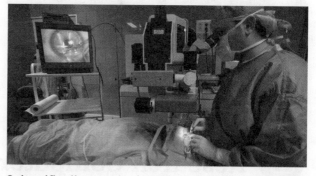

Scientific discoveries with lasers led to LASIK eye correction surgery. It changes the shape of the cornea, your eye's outer covering. After surgery, people may not need glasses or contacts.

11. How did science contribute to better meet people's vision wants and needs?

_____

_____

_____

Science with Vision

Glasses, contacts, and LASIK vision correction are all great examples of how scientific discoveries with optics help many people see better. Many scientific discoveries are helped with tools. New tools designed by engineers may in turn lead to new scientific discoveries.

This refracting telescope is an engineered tool that helps you see things far away by combining lenses. Telescopes are used by astronomers to study objects in space.

This reflecting telescope is an engineered tool that helps you see things far away using mirrors and lenses. These telescopes are also used by astronomers to study objects in space.

A lab microscope is an engineered tool that helps biologists and students like you look at living cells and other tiny objects.

Language SmArts

Research Computer Technology

12. Research online to summarize one scientific discovery that faster, more powerful computers made possible. Make a short presentation of your research to the class.

_____

_____

_____

Thinking Alike

Engineers and scientists use some of the same ways of doing things. Both scientists and engineers see a problem and ask questions about it. They think about the specifics and use models to design a solution. For example, when at first the Hubble telescope was not taking clear images, scientists and engineers worked as a team and discovered that Hubble's main mirror had been built incorrectly. They modeled different solutions on Earth and tested those solutions many times.

NASA engineers used evidence from their tests to determine whether their proposed solutions would work. They used math to analyze the solutions, keeping in mind that any Hubble fix would take place in outer space. Throughout the process, NASA scientists and engineers communicated with each other to find the best solutions.

Thinking Differently

Scientists and engineers follow many of the same methods to find answers to problems. However, their goals differ. Scientists, for example, conduct research and investigations to add to our knowledge. An example might be interpreting data from distant galaxies to better estimate when those galaxies formed. Engineers, on the other hand, focus on solving problems or achieving goals.

Although science and engineering have different goals, their work complements one another. Advances in science often lead to advances in engineering, and advances in engineering often lead to advances in science.

New technology can lead to new science. The first personal computers, like this prototype, led to new scientific discoveries.

13. Choose the words from the word bank that correctly complete the sentences.

add to knowledge	make loopholes	make problems	solve a problem
mathematics	no models	problems	solutions

Engineers _____ and scientists _____

_____. They both use _____ and

computational thinking.

Looking at What They Do

The overlapping ways that scientists and engineers do their jobs may seem confusing. Use the question below to summarize the similarities and differences.

14. For each item, circle all that apply in the right column. (Hint: Think about the goals of scientists versus those of engineers.)

Activity	Who does it?
Analyze test data to find the best boat design	Scientist or Engineer
Ask questions to find out if Earth's surface is changing	Scientist or Engineer
Use a model to explain how animals behave	Scientist or Engineer
Plan and carry out a fair test	Scientist or Engineer
Use evidence to argue for the best solution	Scientist or Engineer
Show and explain a new way to build a wall	Scientist or Engineer
Analyze test data to explain how forces affect objects	Scientist or Engineer
Use a model to test a new speaker design	Scientist or Engineer
Graph the data gathered during a test	Scientist or Engineer
Use evidence to argue for the best explanation	Scientist or Engineer
Ask questions to see what is wrong with a thermometer	Scientist or Engineer
Read and critique an explanation of plant growth	Scientist or Engineer

 EVIDENCE NOTEBOOK How did scientists and engineers work together on Hubble? Write your answer in your Evidence Notebook.

Putting It Together

15. What do engineers and scientists have in common?

_____

_____

_____

_____

_____

HANDS-ON ACTIVITY
Testing Straw Beams

Objective

Collaborate with your partners to see how different bundles of straws can support or not support different weights. Have you ever wondered how much weight an object can support by itself? What about if there are 2 or 3 of the same object together. Can they support more?

What question will you investigate to meet this objective?

_____

_____

_____

Materials
- straws (4 per group)
- masking tape
- 2 stacks of books
- 1 foam cup
- paper clip
- string, 20 cm
- pennies or other unit weights
- ruler

Procedure

STEP 1 Begin by setting up your stacks of books. Make sure that they are the same height and at less than one straw length apart. They also must be tall enough to hang a cup beneath.

STEP 2 Talk with your partner about what you might think will happen. Discuss how many weights you think one straw can support.

_____

_____

STEP 3 Tie the string to make a loop. Use the paper clip and tape to put a hook on the cup. Check that the paper clip can hook onto the string loop. Check that the paper clip will support at least 50 weights.

STEP 4 Begin measuring by passing a straw through the string loop. Then place the single straw across the stack of books. Carefully hang the cup on the string. Add weights one by one until the straw bends and falls.

STEP 5 Tape an additional straw to the original straw and hook the cup on the straw bundle. Slowly add weights one by one until the straw bundle bends and falls.

STEP 6 Repeat Step 4 until your team has built and tested a straw bundle using four straws in all.

Record your data below.

Number of straws	1	2	3	4
Washers supported				

What else did you notice while testing the straw bundles?

_____

_____

_____

Analyze Your Results

STEP 7 Summarize your results below. Tell which bundle of straws supported the most and which the least. Find two other groups and compare your results. Explain any differences.

_____

_____

_____

_____

STEP 8 Make a bar graph to record your measurements. Use your bar graph to interpret your results.

Make a rule based on the information you have gathered.

_____

_____

_____

Draw Conclusions

STEP 9 Why do you think that more straws taped together helped support the weight of the cup?

_____

_____

_____

_____

STEP 10 If you could do the activity again and change two things, what would they be? Why?

_____

_____

_____

_____

_____

STEP 11 If you used a pencil instead of a straw, how do you think that would have changed the results in the experiment? Why?

_____

_____

_____

_____

STEP 12 How could what you learned in this activity be used in building? What questions would you have to answer?

_____

_____

_____

Using Math and Measurement

How Math Helps

You've measured the supporting strength of the straws. You also made a rule to describe how the straws behaved. This is an example of how math can be used to model real-world behavior. Having this type of data allows engineers and scientists to explore and make designs and solutions.

It is important to know how to use math when you are an engineer and scientist because it can help describe objects and systems. Math helps explain and model how these systems work.

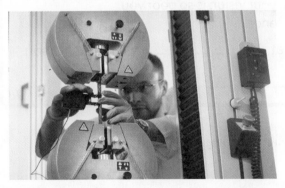

This radar gun helps coaches and fans track the speed of baseball pitches.

A lens gathers and refracts light. Math can describe how the light bends.

This tool measures how much stretching force steel can withstand. This property is tensile strength.

These solar cells capture energy from the sun. The meter measures how much energy is transformed to electricity.

16. How could you use numbers to describe how your classroom changes during the course of a day?

_____

_____

_____

Orbiting Eyeglasses

Math and measuring errors gave the Hubble blurry vision. During manufacturing, the main mirror of the Hubble telescope was ground to the wrong shape by a tiny amount. This error was enough to blur Hubble's view into space. Because the mirror could not be reshaped back on Earth, the best way to fix it was to correct the "eye" of the telescope in space by adding optics that acted like human eyeglasses.

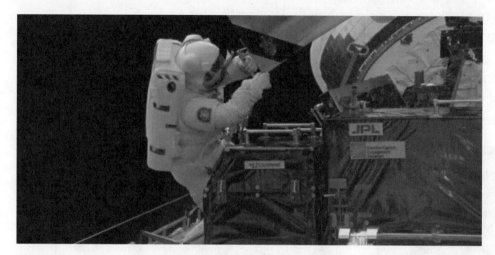

Scientists and engineers worked together to build a solution to correct the Hubble telescope's "vision."

The solution involved using a set of devices that corrected for the flaw in the mirror. These devices were developed and tested on Earth.

Do the Math
The Eyes Have It

17. A person with healthy eyesight has 20/20 vision. If you have 20/100 vision, it means that what healthy eyes can see at 100 feet, your vision is so poor you can only see at 20 feet. Complete the following sentence.

If someone has 20/10 vision, what others see at _____ feet, that person

can see at _____ feet, which is _____ than normal.

EVIDENCE NOTEBOOK Record how eyeglasses improve the vision of three different people you know.

Putting It Together

18. How did science, math, and engineering together repair the Hubble telescope?

_____

_____

_____

Discover More

Check out this path . . . or go online to choose one of these other paths.

Careers in Science & Engineering

- **Music and Math**
- **Moore's Law**

Computer Science

Explore Online

Have you ever wondered how computers work? Who helps design them? Software engineers work hard to design and create the software for computers. You can think of the software as the "chores" list for a computer. By combining many, many instructions, software can do complex things, such as modeling the solar system or playing a game.

Once the software is written, people can use the software in their computers.

A software engineer works with computers all the time.

Software engineers are important for designing software models and solutions. These solutions then help other people use computers to solve problems as well.

19. Go online and research software for modeling. Use the space below to identify the software and describe what it can be used to do.

_____

_____

_____

Software engineers need to know how to use and understand different kinds of computer code. This is a simple program in a language called BASIC.

20. Now, research online for a short lesson on how to code software. Describe it.

_____

_____

_____

Software engineers make computer models that are used by NASA scientists to plan the missions of spacecraft to answer specific questions about travel to planets, moons, and asteroids in our solar system. Data such as the date of launch, the size of the spacecraft, its speed, and the length of the mission are entered into the computer model. The model maps multiple paths in space for the spacecraft, and helps scientists and engineers determine the best flight plan for the spacecraft.

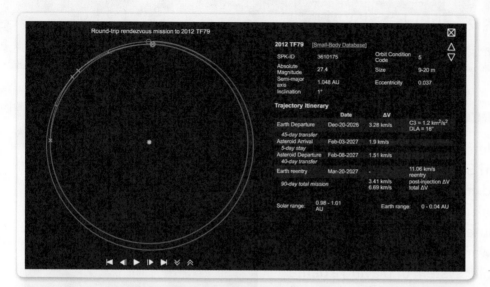

This computer model shows a 90-day space mission to an object passing near Earth.

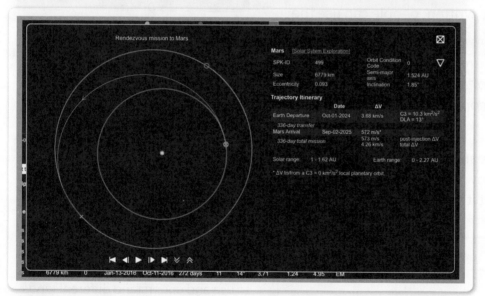

This computer model shows plans for a mission to Mars.

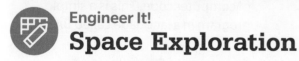

Engineer It!

Space Exploration

21. How can computer models be used to expand space exploration?

_____

_____

_____

Lesson Check

Name _____

Can You Solve It?

1. Use what you have learned to explain how scientists and engineers worked to fix the Hubble telescope. Be sure to do the following:

   • Explain how scientists and engineers identified the problem.

   • Describe the solution that was developed to repair Hubble.

   • Identify how scientists and engineers worked together to fix Hubble.

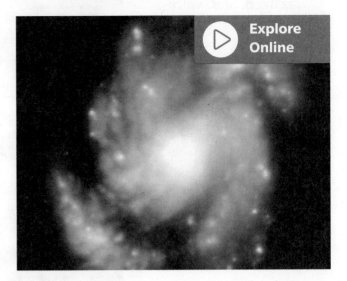

Explore Online

EVIDENCE NOTEBOOK Use the information you've collected in your Evidence Notebook to help you cover each point above.

_____

_____

_____

_____

_____

_____

_____

_____

Checkpoints

2. Which of the following are examples of key practices for scientists and engineers? Circle all that apply.

   a. composing music

   b. arguing in court

   c. analyzing and interpreting

   d. designing solutions based on models

   e. asking questions

3. Organize each image to sort out how the Hubble telescope was fixed. Start with evidence of the problem.

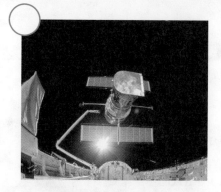
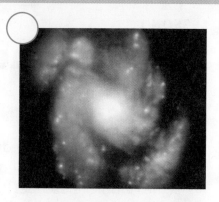

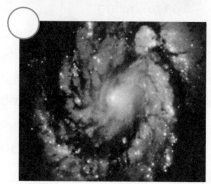

4. Match each idea with its concept.

Scientist

Engineer

Solve problems

Gain knowledge

5. How is mathematics used in science and engineering? Circle all that apply.

   a. in estimating materials and costs   **c.** to analyze data

   b. in measurements   **d.** to use technology

6. Which of the following are examples of technology? Check all that apply.

   a. tree   **d.** dog

   b. calculator   **e.** pet leash

   c. lamp

Lesson Roundup

Circle all that apply.

A. It is the job of engineers to
1. discover how natural things work.
2. apply technology.
3. develop solutions.
4. eliminate technology.
5. improve solutions.

B. Define technology. What are some examples of it around us?

_____

_____

_____

C. Which of the following describes the field of science that helped fix the Hubble telescope?
1. geology
2. optometrists
3. bulldozing
4. optics

D. Choose the words from the word bank to complete the sentences.

weird	similar	data	plants	solutions engineers	conclusions

Engineers and scientists work in _____ ways. Both make sure to use

_____ to help them form _____.

E. Circle all phrases that are examples of engineers applying math to their work.
1. a pie graph showing the different types of food in the cafeteria
2. the angle of the ramp leading to a gym
3. an equation that describes the arc of a basketball in the air
4. your calculator

What Is the Design Process?

Hiking is a wonderful way to experience the natural world. Trails also affect the environment, though. Sometimes people have to make changes to minimize or avoid damage.

By the end of this lesson . . .
you'll be able to use the engineering design process to find a good solution to this problem.

Can You Solve It?

 **Explore Online**

You are a ranger walking in your park. As you get closer to High Top Hill, it's getting harder to walk uphill because there's a deep trench worn in the path, and some of the soil on the path seems to be washed away. How could you solve this problem?

1. What do you think a good solution would look like? What would you need to do before you start to build? What are some things that would limit your design? How would you know if your solution was successful?

_____

_____

_____

_____

_____

 EVIDENCE NOTEBOOK Look for this icon to help you gather evidence to answer the questions above.

Defining a Problem

It's All in the Details

Once you have a problem, you need to learn more about it before you can get started on a solution. Let's continue with the problem of building or repairing a path up the steep High Top Hill in the park. What would you want to know before you started to design the path? You might want to know about the following:

- weather in this area
- features of the area
- materials you can use
- time you have to build

Learning more about the topic is a best way to make good decisions about what you want to do. This additional knowledge helps you to define the criteria you will use and also determine any constraints. **Criteria** tell the desirable features of a solution. For your path, you need to make sure the path is safe, reduces erosion, and uses minimal materials.

A **constraint** is something that limits what you are trying to do. This could include limited money to spend, materials, space to build, or time to finish.

2. Identify each item as criteria or constraint by drawing a line to the correct word. Think about how path length interacts with other choices.

cost

| Criteria | availability of materials | Constraints |

keeps people safe

length of path

time

reduces washing away of soil

What Do You See?

Studying a map of the park where you want to build the path is a great way to gather additional information to determine what criteria you will use and any constraints there are.

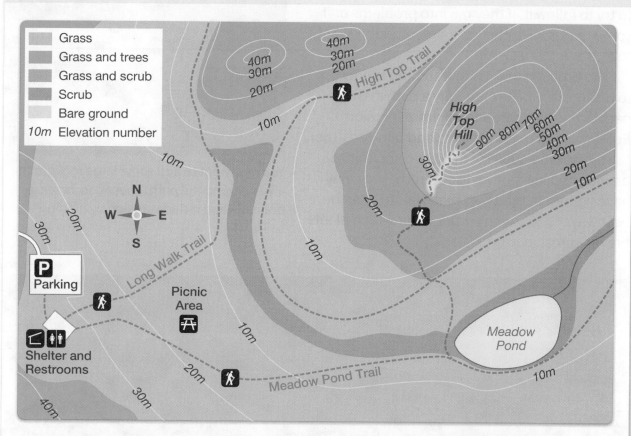

3. This map shows the steep part of High Top Hill where the path will be built or repaired. The topographic lines (contours) show the hills and flat areas. The color key shows plants. Icons show the physical features of the park, such as picnic areas and restrooms.

4. What features of the map are most useful for your planning? Why?

_____

_____

_____

_____

_____

In the Background

To solve a problem, it is often helpful to do some background research to see what is already known about it. If another solution worked somewhere else, then you may want to try to follow it. If they ran into problems or if some things have changed, you probably want to try something else.

The problem you are researching is how to design and make or modify a path in the park that will be safe and minimize erosion. **Erosion** happens when wind and rain carry the soil away. What types of things do you think previous builders have discovered? They may have figured out the best materials to use, the best ways to stay within budget, or which plants prevent erosion.

You may want to add some large rocks to the areas around the path. These can increase drainage and reduce erosion by holding the soil in place.

Plants can be used to prevent erosion. Their roots hold soil in place. Plants that are native to the area are usually best.

Using straw bundles or mulch will help to prevent erosion. This keeps the soil moist. Moist soil erodes less easily than dry soil.

Using some form of barrier is also a good way to prevent erosion. A low wooden or concrete wall slows water flow. Slower flow erodes less soil.

If you build a wall, you also need to design a way for rainfall to drain away. A drainage channel allows the water to flow down the hill where you want it to instead of pooling behind the wall.

5. What other effects of these erosion controls might you need to consider for a park setting?

_____

_____

_____

 EVIDENCE NOTEBOOK What background information can you collect that would be useful in deciding how to build the path on the hill? Enter your answers in your Evidence Notebook.

Glow Images

Put Your Heads Together

Once you have decided on a problem to solve, it is important to gather as many ideas as possible before deciding how you will go about solving the problem. This is a process called **brainstorming.** When you brainstorm, you collect as many different ideas as you can, no matter how good you think they are. This technique is especially useful when working with a group of people.

a. First, generate as many ideas as you can in 5–10 minutes. Listen to everyone's ideas without judging. Select one person to serve as the recorder. Using a whiteboard everyone can see is very helpful.

b. Next, discuss the ideas as a group. Give each person a chance to explain what they meant.

c. After all the ideas are discussed, eliminate any ideas that do not meet the constraints (limits) of the problem. Narrow the list down to two or three ideas. Use the decision matrix on the next page to choose which idea to develop further.

6. Why does brainstorming work best with a group?

_____

_____

_____

_____

Make a Decision Matrix

7. Engineers use a decision matrix to determine which solution is best, given the criteria of the problem. List the criteria in the left column and assign a priority by choosing a number from 1 (low priority) to 5 (top priority). List the top ideas for solving the problem across the top. Rate each solution by giving it a number of points for each criterion. If it fully meets that criterion, give it the maximum number of points. If it only partly meets that criterion, give it fewer points. Add up the points to help you make a decision.

Criteria	Priority (1–5)	Solutions		
		A	B	C
Total points				

Language SmArts

Background Research

8. Learning the details of a project through research is a good first step before brainstorming possible solutions. Also use several sources to conduct some brief research on the design solutions from the brainstorming session. Summarize what you learn in the box below.

Tip

The English Language Arts Handbook can provide help with understanding how to research, using several sources.

_____

_____

HANDS-ON ACTIVITY

Testing a Path with a Scale Model

Objective

Collaborate with a team to build a scale model of the problem to get a better understanding of how your solution might work or even if it will work.

In this activity, you will build a model of High Top Hill to test the solution you have chosen to develop further. If you find your initial idea does not work well, you may decide to change your solution.

What problem will you investigate to meet this objective?

_____

_____

_____

_____

Possible Materials

- topographic map
- clay and soil
- craft sticks
- paint tray or large pan
- paper and cardboard
- plastic bricks
- plastic wrap or foil
- ruler
- watering can or sprayer

Procedure

STEP 1 Obtain the topographic and physical features map from your teacher, and take a good look at the area of High Top Hill where you want to build the path.

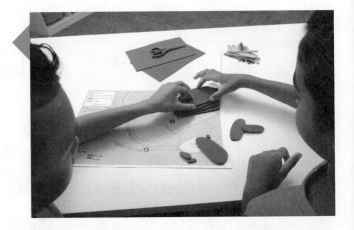

Do these two types of maps tell you everything you need to know about the park? Is there another kind of map that would be helpful?

_____

_____

_____

STEP 2 Use the materials provided to construct a model of the hill. Use the maps you just studied to help determine height and other features of the hill. Before you build your solution, test the hill as it is. Spray or drizzle water over it and observe where the water flows.

What types of things could you use to represent the soil, grass, and other plants you need to study?

_____

_____

_____

STEP 3 Apply the path erosion solution your team has brainstormed to the model. Use the ruler to measure the path. You want to be sure that it is not too long, too short, or too steep.

Why is the length of the path an important thing to know for this project?

_____

_____

_____

_____

STEP 4 Use the sprayer or watering can to slowly drizzle water on your model hill with the solution in place. Be sure to notice the directions it flows in as it goes from the top to the bottom. Record your findings. These should include a picture of your hill design, location of the path, and the flow of the water.

What does the water represent? Does it flow as you want it to?

_____

_____

_____

_____

STEP 5 Adjust your erosion solution as necessary. You want to be sure that the water coming down the hill does not erode the path or the soil around it. Then improve and retest your erosion solution.

Why might you need to move the location of the path?

_____

_____

_____

_____

Turn in your findings to your teacher. Be sure to keep a copy of them for yourself.

Analyze Your Results

STEP 6 If your scale model is 10 centimeters and the actual path is 100 times as long, how many meters is the actual path?

_____

STEP 7 Why is the length of the path an important thing to know?

_____

_____

_____

_____

_____

STEP 8 What questions do you have about the process of solving engineering problems?

_____

_____

_____

_____

_____

_____

_____

_____

STEP 9 Sketch and label your solution. Then explain how it works.

Draw Conclusions

STEP 10 What changes did you have to make to your path design after pouring the water? Why?

_____

_____

STEP 11 How well will your erosion solution prevent erosion?

_____

_____

STEP 12 What difficulties do you think you may encounter in building the path that your team proposed?

_____

_____

_____

Choosing the Best Solution

Zeroing In

How often do you get things perfect on the first try? It often takes many trials before a working solution is found. The important thing to remember is that having to do something over does not mean you have failed. It just means you have found a way something will not work. The old phrase, "If at first you do not succeed, try, try again" works well in engineering.

Engineering design improves as you test design ideas and make improvements. Each trial gives you more information. Over time, you will develop a prototype that meets all the criteria. It's also important to test several times. If something happens once during a test, it might just be a chance event. If it happens many times, you can rely on it more.

9. How does repeating tests and building on your successes lead to better solutions?

_____

_____

_____

_____

_____

_____

_____

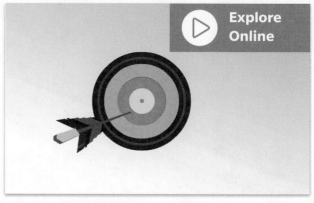

Explore Online

a. The first shot lands on the target a little too low and to the left of the bull's-eye. How would you hold the bow differently?

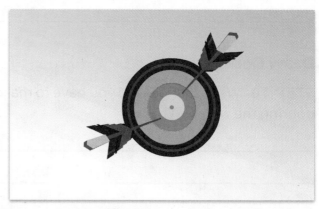

b. On the second try, the arrow is a little too high and to the right of the bull's-eye. How would you hold the bow differently this time?

c. Bull's-eye! You hit the target right in the center. Repeating tests and making improvements each time is important.

Collaborating and Communicating

10. In the previous Apply What You Know, you brainstormed ideas with your team about how to design and build the path to minimize erosion and improve safety. In this activity, you will visit two other teams in your class to see what ideas they had about the problem.

   Discuss your initial erosion solutions and how they changed after the first test.

   Be sure to take notes and summarize them, describing what would be the ideal solution to the problem. Be prepared to share your summary with the class.

_____

_____

_____

_____

_____

_____

11. Choose the correct words to complete each sentence. You can use each word more than once.

often	improved	rarely	repeated	testing

Design solutions are _____ perfect at first. Through

_____ trials, they can be _____. The kinds

of improvements that need to be made can be determined by

_____.

 EVIDENCE NOTEBOOK In your Evidence Notebook, explain why testing different solutions to the problem of erosion on the park path would help improve the final design solution.

39

It's a Process

As you have in this lesson, engineers follow a loose set of steps to develop solutions. The steps are a *design process* or an *engineering design process.* The steps may blend together or repeat. The steps can be sorted into three parts—defining the problem, developing a solution, and improving and retesting.

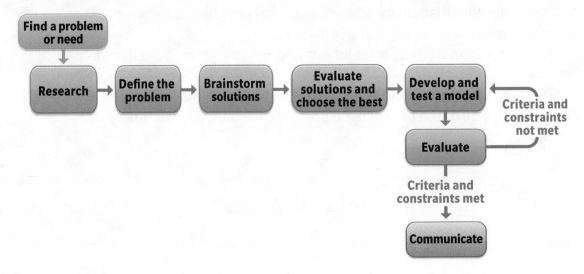

12. Sort the engineering steps into the categories below.

Define the problem	Develop solutions	Record, improve, and retest

Putting It Together

13. Why is collaboration such an important part of the design process? Give an example from your recent Hands-On Activity.

_____

_____

_____

_____

_____

Discover More

Check out this path . . . or go online to choose one of these other paths.

| People in Science & Engineering | • Appalachian Trail Maintenance
• A Trail Erosion Problem |

Wangari Maathai

Explore Online

Wangari Maathai was a scientist, college professor, and environmentalist who educated the world about the impact of erosion and deforestation. Born in Kenya and educated in the United States and Germany, she earned a doctoral degree (PhD). She dedicated her life to preserving the environment by planting trees.

In Kenya, there is limited space that can be used for farming because most of the soil lacks nutrients. Farmers cut down the trees to plant their crops where there are enough nutrients. This is called **deforestation**. When the trees are gone, rains and winds can carry the soil away. This is erosion. Dr. Maathai worked tirelessly to educate the people of her country about harmful deforestation.

Dr. Wangari Maathai was a professor, scholar, author, and avid environmentalist. Her work with the Green Belt Movement earned her the Nobel Peace Prize in 2004.

14. Why might deforestation cause erosion?

_____

_____

_____

_____

_____

_____

Impact in Kenya

Erosion and deforestation in Kenya were two engineering problems that the Green Belt Movement was designed to solve. The engineering design process could be applied to large problems like this. Just like smaller problems, there are constraints that limit the solutions to these problems. For example, the local climate, the availability of young trees, and the amount of money available all affected the Green Belt Movement. There are criteria that help measure success. Often, a large problem such as this is solved as a series of smaller problems.

15. Suppose you had to plant lots of trees but could not afford to buy them from a nursery. What would you do?

_____

_____

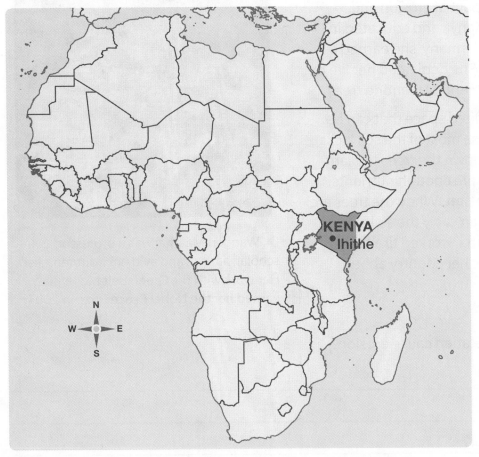

Dr. Maathai did her work in Kenya, located on the continent of Africa. What is the environment like here? Most of the country is very dry. Planting trees helps clean the air and bring in more water to the area.

16. Propose criteria for success for the Green Belt Movement.

_____

_____

Lesson Check

Name _____

Can You Solve It?

1. Now that you have learned more about the engineering design process, how would you make a good erosion solution that also makes it safe to walk down the path? Be sure to do the following:

- Define some of the criteria and constraints related to this problem and solution.

- Describe how brainstorming and researching other erosion solutions helped come up with a good solution.

- Explain how testing, improving, and retesting helped you develop an erosion solution.

EVIDENCE NOTEBOOK Use the information you've collected in your Evidence Notebook to help you cover each point.

_____

_____

_____

_____

_____

_____

_____

_____

Checkpoints

2. Defining a problem is often the first part of the engineering design processes. Which of these steps are usually part of defining the problem? Select all that apply.
   - **a.** evaluating the design
   - **c.** doing additional research
   - **b.** finding a problem to be solved
   - **d.** testing a solution

3. Draw a line from each item in the middle to sort the items as criteria or constraints.

time

| Criteria | erosion is reduced | Constraints |

location

the solution is
safe

money

4. Choose the correct words to complete each sentence.

| brainstorming   testing   share   withhold   reduce   expand |

Good _____ techniques include letting every member of the group

_____ their ideas. After all members have spoken, the best thing to do

is _____ the list in order to figure out the best way to solve the problem.

5. Which of the following are true about the engineering design process? Select all that apply.

a. Collaboration and communication never play a role in the design process.

b. Each step needs to be followed in an exact order.

c. Sometimes steps are repeated or blend together.

d. Some solutions work better than others.

e. The steps are always the same, no matter what the problem.

6. Why is communication important in the engineering design process? Choose all that apply.

a. Engineers want to know what mistakes others have made.

b. to ensure that brainstorming happens after the experiment is designed

c. to share information about different discoveries

d. Engineers need it to keep track of where others are living.

Lesson Roundup

A. Your teacher wants the class to brainstorm ways to rearrange the desks in class so everyone can see the front of the class better. Arrange the steps of the process you would use.

Ask questions to learn more about the problem. _____

Decide which solutions best met the criteria and constraints. _____

Assign someone to record the class's ideas. _____

Identify constraints and criteria for a good solution. _____

Discuss the ideas to reduce the number of possible solutions. _____

Test the solution to see if the problem has been solved. _____

B. Choose the correct words for each sentence.

problem	conclusion	background research	more brainstorming
solutions	criteria	constraints	brainstorming

After a _____ has been identified, it is important to do

_____ to learn as much as possible about the issue.

This will lead to more complete set of _____ and

_____. Once all these factors are in place,

the solution can be designed.

C. What role does research play in the design solution process?

_____

_____

_____

How Does Technology Affect Society?

In the mid 20th century, American drivers liked their cars to look like the jet planes and rockets of the era.

By the end of this lesson . . .
you'll understand how and why technology changes over time.

Can You Solve It?

Look at this car! It was designed and built more than 50 years ago. It has some features that are similar to those of today's cars, but it also has some features that are very different. Look at the back of the car. These fins were designed to mimic the look of fighter jets and rockets of the time. Cars today look very different from this. What do you think led to this change?

1. Why have cars lost their fins and changed in other ways over time?

_____

_____

_____

_____

_____

_____

_____

Tip

Learn more about technology by reading *How Are Science and Math Used in Engineering?* **and** *What Is the Design Process?*

 EVIDENCE NOTEBOOK Look for this icon to help you gather evidence to answer the question above.

Improving Over Time

So Many Changes!

Fins are just one way that cars from the 1950s differ from today's cars. Many of the changes show how society's needs and wants have changed over time. For example, people want cars that are comfortable, easier to drive, and have more safety features. Look at the images to learn more about ways that the design of automobiles has changed over time.

In the 1950s, people wanted cars that resembled fast flying machines. Today, cars have a much more streamlined, rounded shape. The streamlined shape reduces drag between the car and the air. This increases the car's fuel efficiency, or how far it can go using a certain amount of fuel.

Features inside the car have also changed over time. Modern dashboards still provide information about the car, such as its speed and remaining fuel. But they also have systems for entertainment and navigation. These often depend on connections to satellites, radio towers, or cell phone towers.

Safety in automobile engineering is influenced by society in two ways: choices people make and regulations put in place by the government. In the 1950s, seat belts were not required. In the 1960s, the federal government required all cars to have seat belts. Later, laws were passed requiring people to use them.

When a car stops suddenly, the driver is in danger of hitting the steering wheel. Today's steering wheels contain airbags, which inflate quickly when a car is in an accident. The airbag acts as a cushion. Since 1998, government regulations have required airbags in cars.

2. Select one of the sets of images. Summarize how that part of the automobile changed. Based on the trend you observed, predict a future change that you think might occur in this automobile part. Explain why you made this prediction.

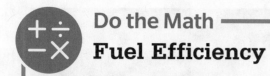
3. The main job of a car is to get people or things from one place to another. Cars use fuel, such as gasoline, to do so. Fuel efficiency is a measure of how much fuel it takes to go a certain distance. The term *gas mileage*, or just *mileage*, is sometimes used to describe a car's fuel efficiency. Some people want cars that are very fuel efficient. These cars use fewer resources and reduce the costs associated with running the car because the driver spends less money on fuel.

Analyze this graph of the average fuel efficiency for different types of vehicles. Identify the trend you see for each vehicle type.

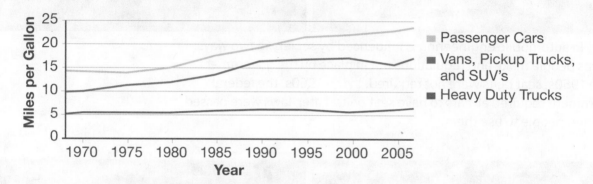

Make a rough copy of the graph in your notebook, leaving room on the right. Use online resources to find mileage figures for modern vehicles of each type. Add the highest and lowest values you find to the graph.

Type of vehicle	Miles per gallon	
	Highest	Lowest
Heavy duty trucks		
Vans, pickup trucks, and SUVs		
Passenger cars		

4. What trends did you identify in the graph? Does the range of data you found through online research support the argument that the trends will continue? What evidence do you have to support this argument?

_____

_____

_____

_____

_____

_____

Fuel can be expensive. Operating a fuel-efficient car can lead to big savings at the gas pump.

 EVIDENCE NOTEBOOK In your Evidence Notebook, identify and describe ways in which society has caused changes in the design of cars over time. Enter your answers in your Evidence Notebook.

 Language SmArts
Compare and Contrast

5. You have learned about some ways that cars have changed since the 1950s. You have also gathered information about some of the factors that caused these changes. Select one other specific design feature or part of a car, such as tires or brakes. Use print or digital sources to gather information about ways in which that aspect of car design has changed over time. Find out what factors influenced or caused these changes. Write a summary of what you learn.

Tip

The English Language Arts Handbook can provide help with understanding how to compare and contrast.

_____

_____

_____

_____

_____

_____

_____

_____

Consequences

What's the Impact?

New technologies cause changes. Some of the changes are positive changes. Other changes caused by new technology are negative. Engineers and designers think about changes that a new technology might cause. They discuss and evaluate expected changes. Technology can also cause unexpected changes or consequences.

Like any technology, cars have caused positive and negative changes. Widespread availability of cars makes it possible for people to travel quickly over much greater distances. They change where people live and work. They also change the shape of cities and the typical look of houses. Look at the images to learn more about positive and negative changes caused by cars.

Positive

Cars can be used to get people where they need to go. Minivans and other larger cars can make transportation more efficient.

Everything from food to building supplies can be transported easily using a car. Minivans and trucks can carry even larger hauls.

Cars make it easy for people to get where they want to go. Whether it's for work or vacation, a car can be used to get there more quickly.

Negative

Most cars on the road today burn fossils fuels. This results in pollution, including a kind of hazy brown air called smog. Air pollution has negative impacts on people's health as well as the local and global environment.

When many people own cars, traffic is a result. Greater amounts of traffic result in an increase in accidents, pollution, and the time people spend trying to get from one place to another.

Shanghai, China

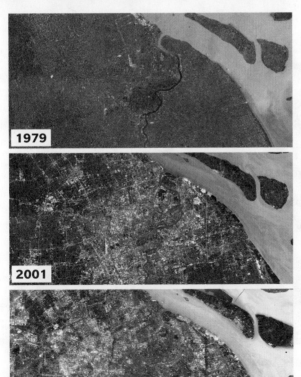

1979

2001

2013

A negative change caused by cars is called "sprawl." Because people can get from one place to another easily, people can live a long way from where they work, shop, or go to school. Cities get wider as people move further away from the places they need to get to. Traffic, resource use, and pollution increase as a result.

Images

Unexpected Effects

Some aspects of modern living have ended up seeming like negatives after initially seeming like good ideas.

The design of homes has changed as the result of the invention of the car. Garages are now a common part of many houses. When people get home and pull their car directly into a garage, opportunities for talking to neighbors and building community decrease.

As people spend more time in their cars, they get less physical activity. This has a negative impact on people's health.

Classifying Effects

You've just read about the effects of cars and car-related technologies. As you know, the effects of technologies can be positive or negative. They can also be expected or unexpected.

6. Use lines or symbols to classify different car-related effects. Each effect should be either positive or negative, and some may also be classified as surprising.

| Positive effects |
| Negative effects |
| Surprising effects |

| ability to move people and things to where they need to go |
| ability to travel long distances |
| increase in pollution |
| decrease in physical activity |
| increase in sprawl |
| increase in traffic |
| distracting technologies lead to accidents |

 EVIDENCE NOTEBOOK You've learned about some of the different kinds of effects technology can have. In your Evidence Notebook, explain why most technologies have both positive and negative effects.

Putting It Together

7. As automobile engineers evaluate new technologies, they think about the expected effects of those technologies. What do you think would happen if a car-related technology was introduced that had unexpected negative effects?

_____

_____

_____

_____

Car Competition

Objective

Collaborate to design a balloon-powered car. Your team might want it to be fast, safe, able to carry a lot, good looking, or a mix of these.

What problem are you trying to solve?

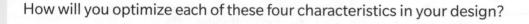

_____

_____

_____

Possible Materials
- balloon
- straws
- toy car or cart
- masking tape
- stopwatch
- egg in sealable plastic bag
- small weights
- scrap cardboard
- scissors
- plastic bottles

Procedure

STEP 1 With your group, discuss the four following features of cars: speed, safety, cargo capacity, and looks. At the conclusion of the activity, all the cars designed by your class will compete in those four categories. Read the description of the competitions. Discuss these criteria and the constraints on your design.

How will you optimize each of these four characteristics in your design?

_____

_____

STEP 2 Work with your group to design your car. Make a sketch or other model of your design.

STEP 3 Build your car. Test your design. Does the car move without you pushing it? If not, make any necessary improvements.

Did the car work as you expected? Are there improvements that could be made?

_____

_____

_____

_____

STEP 4 As a class, carry out the following competitions:

a. Use masking tape to set up a start line and a finish line on a flat surface. Place all of the cars at the start line. Release all of the cars at the same time. Record the time it takes for each car to move from start to finish. Carry out three trials. Average the results. Use the averaged results to determine the fastest car. Record your results.

Car	Time(s)			
	Trial 1	Trial 2	Trial 3	Average

b. Place an equal amount of cargo weight in or on each car. Place each car at the start line, and start the cars. Determine which cars could travel all the way to the finish line with the weight in the car. Use those cars for the next trial. Add equal weight to each of these cars. Repeat the procedure, adding more weight each trial. Continue until only one car can make it from start to finish carrying the weights. This is the car with the greatest cargo capacity. Record your results.

_____

_____

_____

_____

_____

c. Take a class vote to determine which car has the best appearance. Record your results.

_____

_____

_____

_____

_____

d. Place eggs in zippered baggies, then place an egg in each car. Place the cars an equal distance from a barrier, such as a wall. Start the cars. See which cars keep the egg from breaking when they hit the barrier. Repeat this procedure with the cars that had unbroken eggs. Move the barrier closer to the start line until only one car remains. Record your results.

	Winning car
Speed	
Ability to carry cargo	
Looks	
Safety	

Analyze Your Results

STEP 5 What category did your car compete most successfully in? What design features contributed to its success in that category?

_____

_____

_____

_____

STEP 6 Compare your results to the results of other groups. Describe any similarities or differences you notice.

_____

_____

_____

_____

STEP 7 In the real world, consumers choose cars based on their wants and needs. What two characteristics might be most important to a large family that enjoys outdoor sports and has a young baby? What two characteristics might be less important for this family? Why?

_____

_____

_____

_____

Draw Conclusions

STEP 8 Make a claim about whether a single car could win all four competitions. Cite evidence to support your claim.

_____

_____

_____

_____

STEP 9 What other questions do you have about the ways that cars are designed to meet consumers' needs and wants?

_____

_____

_____

_____

Tradeoffs

You Can't Have Everything

In the activity, you designed a car that had certain design features. It might have been fast, or maybe it could carry a lot of cargo. Changing the design to enhance one characteristic probably made the car less competitive in another way. A **tradeoff** involves giving up a quality or feature of a design to gain a different quality or feature.

Recall that technology is developed based on people's needs and wants. Automotive engineers need to think about these criteria as they design cars. They also need to think about regulations, such as safety standards and mileage requirements, as they design cars.

← **better power**   **better mileage** →

For cars that run on gasoline, more power often means fewer miles per gallon of gas. Automotive engineers must think about the tradeoff between engine power and fuel efficiency as they design vehicles.

← **cleaner air**   **better mileage** →

The amount of pollution given off by cars is regulated. A device called a *catalytic converter* can help reduce the amount of pollutants in gasoline and diesel car exhausts. But the device does reduce the car's mileage.

← **better appearance**   **lower cost** →

The appearance of cars varies widely. Some features that improve a car's appearance also increase the cost of the car. Engineers must decide which design features to include as they design a particular model of automobile.

8. Mark an X on each arrow to show how important each feature is. Explain your choices.

_____

_____

A Balancing Act

You've read that tradeoffs are an important part of automobile design. The tradeoff activity you just completed helped you think about some of these. Some choices are made through government regulations. Others are simply a matter of the preference of consumers. Test results and other information can help consumers make decisions about these tradeoffs.

When consumers shop for a car, they are provided with an average mileage for that car. Car manufacturers test the cars they manufacture. The Environmental Protection Agency reviews and double-checks the results of these tests. Knowing a car's mileage helps consumers evaluate their choices.

The Insurance Institute for Highway Safety tests two different areas of safety. First, they evaluate cars to see how safe they keep passengers during a crash. Second, they rate cars based on how they're engineered to avoid or minimize crashes. Some cars have sensors that will activate the brakes if they are going to collide with something.

9. Tradeoffs are not just a part of engineering. They are a part of everyday life. Describe an example of a tradeoff in everyday life.

_____

_____

_____

Give and Take

Because there are tradeoffs in how products are designed, there can be negotiations between a product's seller and his or her customers. Some products, especially cars, can be customized to have or not have a given feature.

 HANDS-ON Apply What You Know

Make That Sale

10. Tradeoffs are something that car buyers think about. Look back at the activity in which you evaluated tradeoffs in car design. Review your thoughts about each of the four tradeoffs described. Write a description of a vehicle that would fit what you wanted for each of the tradeoffs. Then work with a partner to write a script for an advertisement to sell this car. You'll need to think about what your choices mean in terms of features for the car. You also may want to sketch the car. Be ready to perform the script with your partner.

 EVIDENCE NOTEBOOK Think about how cars have changed since the 1950s. In your Evidence Notebook, describe how tradeoffs have played a role in changing car designs.

Putting It Together

11. When people choose a car, they think about tradeoffs. Use this information to explain why car manufacturers typically sell different models of vehicles with different features.

_____

_____

_____

_____

_____

Discover More

Check out this path . . . or go online to choose one of these other paths.

Careers in Science & Engineering

- **Go Further: Self-Driving Cars**
- **Safety Survey**

Safety Engineer

Automotive engineers are people who apply scientific information to the design of cars. They think about ways in which cars can be improved or changed. They might design ways to make cars faster, more fuel efficient, or less expensive to build. A safety engineer designs ways to make vehicles safer.

Automotive engineers must have a college degree. There are many ways an automobile engineer can specialize. An engineer might use a wide variety of tools and technologies during his or her workday.

Explore Online

Many automotive engineers use CAD, or computer assisted design, as they develop ways to improve automobile design.

Making and testing prototypes like this is an important part of any design process, including the design of cars. Automotive engineers and safety engineers can use prototypes to test and modify their ideas.

The Right Hire

Suppose that you work with a team of engineers that know about how to make a fast car that handles well and looks good. You need someone to help make sure it's as safe as possible. Make a list of things that a safety engineer needs to know in order to make a good member of your team. Explain the types of design decisions that will need to be made based on what you know about tradeoffs in automobile design. Submit your list to your teacher.

The best way for automotive engineers to test their products is to put them into real-life situations, including collisions. To test a windshield's strength, for example, it can be struck by objects that might strike a windshield in a real-world accident.

12. Describe a product in your home that has a design flaw. Suggest a solution.

_____

_____

_____

_____

_____

Lesson Check

Name _____

Can You Explain It?

1. Now that you've learned more about how technology affects society, explain why cars have changed over time. Be sure to do the following:

Explore Online

- Explain how society plays a role in changes in car design.
- Describe the kinds of effects changes in technology such as car design can have.
- Explain how tradeoffs play a role in automotive design and technology.

> **EVIDENCE NOTEBOOK** Use the information you've collected in your Evidence Notebook to help you cover each point.

_____

_____

_____

_____

_____

_____

_____

_____

_____

Checkpoints

2. Which of the following describe(s) ways that cars have changed since the 1950s? Choose all that apply.

   a. They now have airbags.

   b. They no longer include seat belts.

   c. They have a smoother shape.

   d. They get fewer miles per gallon of gasoline.

3. How has the fuel efficiency of cars changed since the 1950s? Choose the correct answer.

    a. It has increased.

    b. It has decreased.

    c. It has stayed the same.

4. This image shows how sprawl has changed a city. Which of the following explains why sprawl is considered a negative change? Choose all that apply.

    a. It causes increased pollution.

    b. It increases the amount of time people spend in the car.

    c. It increases the amount of fuel people use.

    d. It increases the fuel efficiency of cars.

    e. It makes it easier for people to get to the places they need to go.

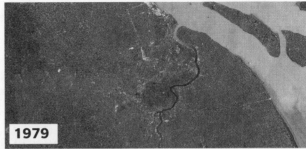

1979

2001

2013

5. Which of these is a positive effect of many people having cars? Choose the correct answer.

    a. It is easier for people to get from place to place.

    b. The amount of air pollution has increased.

    c. The design of homes has changed.

    d. People get less physical activity.

6. Which is the correct definition of a tradeoff? Choose the correct answer.

    a. giving up one feature to gain another

    b. changing a design feature due to people's needs

    c. making sure a design gives people everything they want

    d. adding many features to a design

Lesson Roundup

A. Use lines to assign each of the car features to the era in which they were common.

lower fuel efficiency

tail fins

no seat belts or just lap belts

higher fuel efficiency

streamlined body shape

air bags

| 1950s |

| Now |

B. What is another factor that has led to changes in technology?

_____

_____

C. Choose the correct words to complete each sentence.

Technology can have a variety of effects. Changes that people

think about ahead of time are _____ effects.

Some technologies have good, or _____, effects.

Other technologies have bad, or _____, effects. Most

technologies have a combination of these kinds of effects.

> expected
> unexpected
> positive
> negative

D. An arrow pointing in both directions can be used to show a tradeoff. Explain the tradeoff shown in this image.

better appearance ←——————————→ lower cost

_____

_____

_____

ENGINEER IT!
Lunch Line Lifehack

Suppose that students at your school keep showing up late for their first after-lunch classwork. The reason turns out to be that they're standing too long in the lunch line. So your principal announces a contest: Design a new line that will make things move faster. The winner will be allowed to cut to the front of the lunch line for the rest of the year. You're entering, of course.

Um, could we speed this up a little?

FIND A PROBLEM: How will you know that you have accomplished your goal?

_____

_____

_____

Review the checklist at the end of this Unit Performance Task. Keep those requirements in mind as you proceed.

RESEARCH: Examine the flow of students during lunch. What factors contribute to delays in the lunch line?

_____

_____

_____

BRAINSTORM: Brainstorm two or more ideas with your team for improving each factor you've listed.

_____

_____

_____

_____

_____

List at least three criteria and three constraints for this task.

Criteria	Constraints
_____	_____
_____	_____
_____	_____
_____	_____

MAKE A PLAN: Make a plan by considering your ideas separately and together. Ask yourself the following:

1. Does this idea contribute to accomplishing our goal? How?

2. Which of our ideas fit well together?

3. How do we decide which ideas to keep and which to discard?

_____

_____

_____

DESIGN AND BUILD: Make a labeled diagram that shows how your lunch line design looks and operates.

EVALUATE AND REDESIGN: Test your design. How well does it work, and how do you know? What parts could you improve? How?

_____

_____

✅ Checklist

Review your project and check off each completed item.

_____ Includes a clear goal statement

_____ Identifies factors to be addressed and lists ways to address them

_____ Includes a detailed diagram with explanatory text

_____ Tests the effectiveness of the plan and identifies improvements

_____ Displays and clearly explains the plan

Unit Review

1. What is one reason that this object is used in orbit instead of on the ground? Circle the correct answer.

   a. to avoid collision with objects on the ground

   b. to provide a clearer view of objects in outer space

   c. to keep starlight from distorting photographic images

   d. to relay radio signals without atmospheric interference

Hubble Space Telescope

2. Which of the following is true of technology but not true of nature? Circle all that apply.

   a. Technology can be studied.

   b. Technology is constantly changing.

   c. Technology is produced by humans.

   d. Technology is found everywhere on Earth.

   e. Technology uses science and mathematics.

3. Underline the text that correctly completes each sentence.

   Engineers

   a. discover things about the world and universe.

   b. use scientific discoveries to develop technology.

   Scientists

   c. discover things about the world and universe.

   d. use scientific discoveries to develop technology.

4. Which feature of this vintage car's brake light meets a need instead of a want?

   a. the shiny chrome frame

   b. the red lens

   c. the color of the paint

   d. the rounded shape

5. You have been assigned the project of making the object shown above.
Write in the blanks to classify the statements below as criteria (CR) or constraints (CO).

_____ You must spend no more than $25 on materials.

_____ The project must be able to withstand strong wind.

_____ The object should be lightweight.

_____ The project must be completed today.

_____ You must build the project without any help.

_____ You must place the project in a safe location.

6. Scientists and engineers often build _____ models to use in conducting investigations or performing experiments.

7. Using the numbers 1–5, label these steps of a possible engineering design process to show their most likely order.

_____ Choose and test the best design.

_____ Modify and retest the design.

_____ Identify a purpose/problem/goal.

_____ Brainstorm possible designs.

_____ Evaluate the test results.

8. Which of the following is a result that comes from the widespread use of cars? Select all that apply.

   a. greater ease of travel

   b. pollution from exhaust fumes

   c. people getting less exercise

   d. greater difficulty in transporting cargo

   e. less efficient long-distance communication

9. Write in the choices that correctly complete the sentences.

> **catalytic converter**   **crash testing**   **mileage testing**   **crumple zone**

A _____ is an example of a car safety feature.

A _____ is an example of a pollution-

reducing feature.

10. Write in the choices that correctly complete the sentence.

> **riders**   **sensors**   **software**   **mirrors**

Driverless cars depend on _____ and _____
to gather and analyze information about the road and surrounding
environment.

72

Matter

▷ **Explore Online**

Unit Project: Conservation of Matter
How can you prove that matter is conserved during a change? You will conduct an investigation with your team. Ask your teacher for details.

Everything you see here is matter: the water, the sand, the air. Matter can change.

At a Glance

74

Vocabulary Game: Picture It

for 3 to 4 players

Materials
- kitchen timer or online computer timer
- sketch pad

How to Play
1. Take turns to play.
2. To take a turn, choose a word from the Word Box. Do not tell the word to the other players.
3. Set the timer for 1 minute.
4. Draw pictures on the sketch pad to give clues about the word. Draw only pictures and numbers. Do not use words.
5. The first player to guess the word gets 1 point. If that player can use the word in a sentence, he or she gets 1 more point. Then that player gets a turn to choose a word.
6. The first player to score 5 points wins.

matter

Anything that takes up space.

boiling point

The point at which matter changes from a liquid to a gas.

Unit Vocabulary

 **boiling point:** The point at which matter changes from a liquid to a gas.

 **melting point:** The temperature at which matter changes from a solid to a liquid.

 **chemical change:** Change in one or more substance, caused by a reaction, that forms new and different substances.

 **mixture:** A combination of two or more different substances in which the substances keep their identities.

 **conservation of matter:** A law that states that matter cannot be made or destroyed; however, matter can change into a new form.

 **physical change:** A change in which the shape or form of the substance changes, but the substance still has the same chemical makeup.

 **freezing point:** The temperature at which matter is changed from a liquid to a solid.

 **physical properties:** Anything that you can observe about an object by using one or more of your senses.

 **matter:** Anything that takes up space.

 **solution:** A mixture that has the same composition throughout because all its parts are mixed evenly.

What Is Matter?

At an open-air market, you can see and hear many different people buying and selling things. There's fresh fruit and vegetables, freshly baked bread, spices, and drinks such as tea, coffee, and milk. Everything you see, hear, taste, touch, and smell is made of matter.

By the end of this lesson . . .
you'll be able to identify and measure matter.

Can You Explain It?

 Explore
Online

You see many different people running around having a good time. These people are made of matter. The matter within them is made of particles too small to be seen.

1. What kinds of matter do you see in the photo above?

_____

_____

_____

_____

_____

_____

 EVIDENCE NOTEBOOK Look for this icon to help you gather evidence to answer the question above.

Matter Is Everything

What Matters about Matter

Where do you find things made of matter? If you can taste, smell, or touch something, it's matter. Anything that takes up space is **matter**. It can come in different forms and can behave in many different ways. Even a breeze is matter, because air takes up space. But some things that exist, such as heat and light, are not matter. Why not? They don't take up any space.

At the Fair

2. What do the sun, tents, and carnival games have in common?

_____

_____

_____

Matter or Not?

3. Which of the following things are matter? Which are not? Label them as *matter* or *not matter*.

 Explore Online

feelings

_____

food

_____

time

_____

4. What properties do items classified as matter have in common?

_____

_____

5. Which are examples of matter? Sort the items in the word bank into the chart below.

| a candle | a happy thought | light from a lamp |
| air inside of a bubble | a moving ocean wave | ashes from a camp fire |

Matter	Not matter

 EVIDENCE NOTEBOOK There are many types of matter that can be found at the fair. There are also things that cannot be classified as matter. Which things did you see that are considered matter? Why did you select these? Write your responses in your Evidence Notebook.

What Makes Up Matter?

Matter takes up space. But what is it made of? You can break down an object into smaller parts. At first, you can see the broken pieces. Eventually, you would need to use a tool such as a microscope to see the smaller parts. At that stage, the parts can still get smaller, all the way down to their basic particles—the smallest parts of matter that exist.

You cannot see particles, but they make up all matter. The sun, whales, the air, apple juice, and the ink and paper of this page are all forms of matter made of particles.

Contents of Charcoal

6. What kinds of matter do you see here?

Explore Online

_____

_____

Let's explore the particles of the charcoal inside this grill.

Uh-oh. The bag of charcoal has been knocked over. Some of the briquettes have spilled out.

The individual briquette is made of particles that are stuck together.

Even the tiniest speck of a charcoal briquette is made of hundreds of millions of carbon particles like this one.

If a briquette is broken, you can see both large and small parts that make up the whole. Notice how even the smallest particles all look the same. This is because they are made from the same type of matter, called *carbon*.

The piece of charcoal is a form of matter. By zooming in, you can see that the properties of the whole are the same as the properties of the charcoal smaller pieces, from the dust to the particles of carbon.

7. Fill in the blank with the best term: *the same* or *different*.

A large piece of matter has _____ traits as the smaller

pieces and the individual particles of the same matter.

 HANDS-ON Apply What You Know

Is It Still There?

8. In this activity, you will test to see if matter can be destroyed. Your teacher will provide you with a glass of water and a sugar cube. Drop the sugar cube into your glass of water and stir it until it dissolves. Then design a method for determining what happened to it.

How can you test to see what happened to the sugar cube in the water? How can you tell if it is still present or if it disappeared?

_____

_____

_____

Particles, Particles, Everywhere

Remember that matter is made of tiny particles. These particles can rearrange themselves into many different shapes and sizes. But not all matter has a definite shape. Water, milk, and the air you breathe are also forms of matter. It is how these particles join together that determines what kind of matter you have.

Aluminum is a lightweight metal. It is often used to build things that need to move quickly, including cars. The water bottle is made of aluminum.

This cyclist has all the tools he needs to win the big race. The water bottle is made of a material called aluminum, and his shoes and bike have carbon fibers in them. The water in the bottle is made of two different types of particles joined together.

Carbon is a very useful material. It can be found in charcoal in your grill, the sweet tea you drank earlier, and in the soles of the cyclist's shoes.

9. Name something else in the photo. Circle it on the page, and then describe it here.

_____

_____

_____

10. Language SmArts You know that matter can be broken down into smaller and smaller particles. Describe how different particles join together to form other things. Provide an example.

_____

_____

_____

_____

Carbon Fiber

New technologies are always being invented. Carbon fiber is an example. It consists of extremely thin "hairs" that are joined together to form different materials. Because the fibers are so thin, the materials made from them are very lightweight. This property is very useful when designing running shoes or other things that are built for speed.

Carbon fibers are hairlike strings, or sheets, of carbon that can be stuck or woven together to make different materials.

Thanks to carbon fiber, this toy plane is more lightweight, and therefore faster, than a plastic, wooden, or metal toy plane.

11. What are the benefits of using carbon fiber instead of other materials, such as metal, to build machines?

_____

_____

_____

_____

States of Matter

Matter has particular properties. One property of matter is the state in which matter exists. The term *state* refers to how the particles of the matter are behaving. Sometimes scientists call states of matter *phases*.

A *solid* is the state of matter that has definite shape and volume. A solid's particles are tightly packed together and only vibrate in place.

A *liquid* has no definite shape but does have a definite volume. A liquid's particles are not as tightly packed and can flow past each other.

A *gas* has neither definite shape nor definite volume. Its particles have space between them to move freely.

12. Look at the images of matter in different states, and then write down your observations. Focus on shapes and volumes. Do they change?

The shoe consists mainly of different solid materials.

_____

_____

_____

_____

At room temperature, honey is a liquid.

_____

_____

_____

_____

_____

_____

The gas-filled bouncy house can be inflated and deflated by fans.

_____

_____

_____

_____

13. Place the words in the box into the appropriate category, according to the state of matter they're normally found in.

Solid	Liquid	Gas

banana

sailboat

hot cocoa

penny

air

maple syrup

oxygen

HANDS-ON Apply What You Know

Air Is Matter

14. How can you test to see if air has the properties of the state you assigned it to above? Your teacher will give you a glass bowl of water, a plastic cup, and a paper towel.

Pack the paper towel into the bottom of the plastic cup. Hold the cup upside down, with paper towel packed inside, and push it straight down into the bowl all the way to the bottom. Hold it there for a minute, and then pull the cup out the same way it went in—upside down.

What do you notice about the paper towel? Does that prove that air is matter?

Putting It Together

Matter is all around us. It can be broken down from a large size to a small size, but its identity doesn't change. If you add more of the same matter to the original amount of matter, it is still the same substance.

15. What is the difference between a single particle of water and a glass of water?

_____

_____

_____

_____

85

How Much Matter Do You Have?

You already know that all matter has certain properties that make it special. These properties are used to determine what kind of matter you have. Some of these properties can be measured.

Materials
- 2 solid objects
- balance
- beaker
- meterstick
- metric ruler
- unit cubes

Objective

Collaborate to measure two different objects in as many ways as possible with the tools you have. You will be investigating volume, weight, and length.

What question will you investigate to meet this objective?

_____

_____

_____

Procedure

STEP 1 Select two different solid objects to measure, and record what they are in the table below.

Object	Length	Weight	Volume

STEP 2 Determine how you will measure the objects. Plan to measure everything twice for accuracy.

Are there some things you are not able to measure? If so, what?

_____

_____

_____

STEP 3 Use the balance to measure any weight measurements you need to make. Record your measurements in the table with the appropriate unit of measure.

STEP 4 Use a ruler to measure any length measurements you need to make. Record your measurements in the table with the appropriate unit of measure.

STEP 5 Come up with a method to make any volume measurements you need to measure. Record your results in the table with the appropriate unit of measure.

Analyze Your Results

STEP 6 Which object had the greatest volume? What tools did you use to confirm that?

_____

_____

_____

STEP 7 What questions do you have about measuring volume?

_____

_____

Draw Conclusions

STEP 8 Make a claim based on your investigation. Use evidence to support your claim.

_____

_____

_____

Measuring Matter

Making the Meter

When someone asks you how far you live from school, you probably reply with an answer in miles. In science, however, we use metric units such as kilometers, meters, and centimeters to measure length. How did we get from feet and miles to meters and kilometers?

People used feet to measure because it was easy to walk heel to toe in a straight line to find a distance. But people's feet vary in size, which led to disagreements about what a "foot" really was.

A yard was equivalent to 108 barleycorns (a grain) laid end to end. Yardsticks could be cut to this length. A yard had three feet, so a yardstick could be marked to measure feet as well.

In the 1400s, a more standard unit of measure was established. Metals often served as the standards, and copies were made from wood and other less expensive materials.

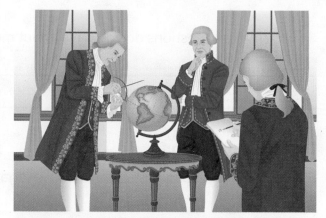

The metric system originated in 18th century France. It uses a decimal-based system. A meter was equal to 1/10,000,000 of the distance from the equator to the North Pole.

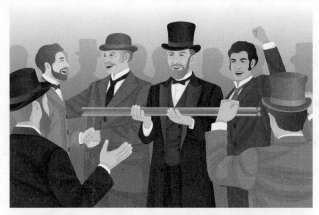

In 1875, a convention was held to establish the meter as the unit of measure. A metal bar was designed that would serve as the standard and wasn't distributed around the world until 1960.

Since the 1980s, light has been used as the measure of a meter. A meter is the distance light travels in a split second ($\frac{1}{299,792,458}$ of a second) when shown in a vacuum.

As you can see, the units of measure for length have changed significantly over time, and we no longer need to argue whose feet are the right size to measure distances.

Do the Math

Measuring Length with the Metric System

16. Measure and record the length, width, and height of your desk in centimeters. Then convert your measurements into meters.

Unit of measure	Length	Width	Height
Centimeters			
Meters			

17. What pattern do you see between your measurements in centimeters and the measurements after you converted them to meters?

_____

_____

_____

Wait for Weight

Another property of matter you have already investigated is weight. Suppose you are measuring how light or heavy an object is. The tools you use to do this are a balance or scale. While most Americans measure weight in pounds, the metric (SI) system uses units called *grams*. The same prefixes are used with weight as are used with length, such as *centi-*, *milli-*, and *kilo-*. With a scale, you might measure a small dog's weight as about 7.5 pounds, which is also 3.4 kg.

A balance can be used to compare the weights of two objects to one another.

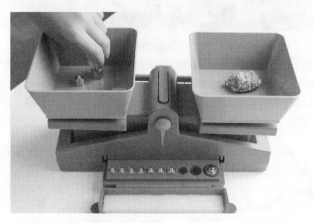
You can use known weights to find the weight of an object on a balance.

18. Find the weights of three things in or near your desk.

Item	Weight

19. How can you use the pan balance to confirm that the heaviest of your objects really was the heaviest?

_____

_____

_____

Scientists and doctors use balances all the time to weigh different things. This vet is measuring the weight of this rabbit to see if it is healthy.

20. Language SmArts Research the meaning of four commonly used prefixes in the metric system. Write an explanation for what each prefix means.

_____

_____

_____

_____

_____

_____

_____

_____

_____

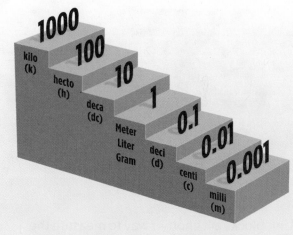

21. Choose the correct words for each sentence.

graduated cylinder	metric ruler	balance
meters	grams	converted	made

A _____ is used to measure weight. Weight can be

measured in _____ . The advantage of the metric

system is that measurements can be easily _____ into

other units.

Measuring Volume

Another property of matter that can be measured is *volume*—the amount of space a given amount of matter takes up. All matter has volume, but sometimes it can be difficult to measure.

If it is a regular shaped object, such as a cube or a box, then you can measure it using a formula: length × width × height. If you take all of these measurements and multiply them together, you will get the volume in cubic units (usually cm^3).

If the object does not have an easy shape to measure, you'll need to use *displacement*. The volume of an object is equal to the volume of water it displaces. If you fill a graduated cylinder or beaker with a known amount of water and drop in your irregular object, you can measure how much the water rises. That displacement is the volume of the object.

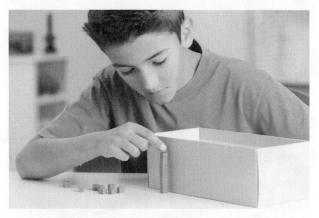

Unit blocks are another way to measure the dimensions of a regular object. This shoebox has many sides of different lengths, so the student uses a different number of cubes to measure each one.

To find the volume, the student needs to find the length, width, and height of the shoebox. Using the cubes is one way of doing this.

22. Someone hands you three apples and asks you for the combined volume of all three. How would you measure this?

_____

_____

_____

_____

_____

 EVIDENCE NOTEBOOK Matter has weight and volume. There are many different methods for measuring these properties. What evidence do you have for this claim? Enter your answer in your Evidence Notebook.

Even if an object whose volume you want to measure has neat, regular sides and an even shape, it may not be practical to stack unit cubes next to or inside the object. A metric ruler may be more practical.

Measuring the length, width, and height in centimeters allows this student to then calculate the volume of the shoebox.

The formula for calculating the volume of the shoebox is length × width × height. This student used the ruler to have more precise results.

23. Find the volumes of three rectangular objects in or near your desk by using unit cubes and a metric ruler.

Item	Volume—unit cubes	Volume—ruler

24. Was there much difference between the volumes measured by unit cubes and the volumes measured with a ruler? Explain.

_____

_____

_____

Solid in Liquid

Some objects do not have the kind of shape that can be measured with rulers. To measure the volumes of such objects, water can be used.

A graduated cylinder is filled with a specific volume of water.

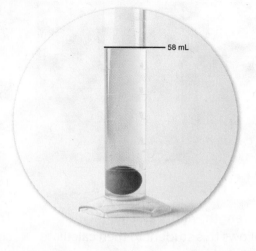

Compare the new water level in the cylinder to the original water level. It shows the volume of the object using displacement.

 HANDS-ON Apply What You Know

How Does Matter Fit Together?

25. Measure out 25 mL of rice using a graduated cylinder. Pour the rice into a container. Then measure out 25 mL of beans. Pour the beans into the same container as the rice. Stir the rice and beans together until they are thorougly mixed. Then pour the combination into the graduated cylinder. Measure the volume. Why is the measurement less than 50 mL?

_____

_____

_____

Putting It Together

26. What properties of matter can you measure? Cite evidence.

_____

_____

_____

Discover More

Check out this path . . . or go online to choose one of these other paths.

Careers in Science & Engineering

- Organizing Particles
- More States of Matter

Materials Scientists and Engineers

Explore Online

Knowing the different properties of matter has allowed for the development of many useful technologies. The scientists who make new materials or improved existing materials are called *materials scientists*. *Materials engineers* take these substances and design new or improved products for us to use. Some of the things materials scientists and engineers have invented include bike helmets, memory foam used in mattresses, and microprocessors used in computers.

Advancements in safety are one way materials scientists and engineers have helped people. Bike helmets are usually made of plastics and other materials that allow air to flow through.

The helmet is also very strong, so it gives a lot of protection to the head. At the same time, it is designed to be weak enough to shatter if an impact is especially strong. This helps prevent the wearer from suffering a concussion.

27. What makes foam a good choice as a material for the inside of a bike helmet?

_____

_____

_____

95

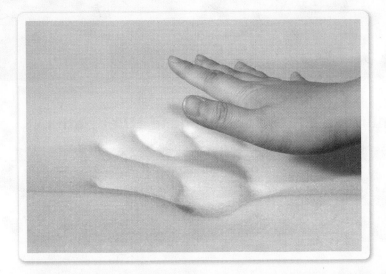

Do you like to jump up and down on your bed? The mattress is most likely made of springs and filling. Memory foam is a new technology that greatly improves comfort for some people when sleeping. When you lay down on the foam, it curves around your body.

What would computers look like if the microprocessor had never been invented? They would still be the size of a large room and be very slow. Knowing the properties of different chemicals allowed materials scientists to invent the tiny chips that are now found in almost all electronic devices.

Think about what other things materials scientists and engineers have invented. Many things you take for granted were once brand new ideas. These things could be invented because people knew about how matter behaves and what its properties are. Maybe someday you can use your knowledge of matter to invent something amazing, too!

28. What properties of matter do you think materials scientists and engineers needed to know to invent memory foam?

_____

_____

_____

_____

_____

Lesson Check

Name _____

Can You Explain It?

1. Now that you've learned more about matter and its different properties, explain how the three main states of matter compare to each other. Be sure to do the following:

   • Name three states of matter.

   • Detail the different motion of particles in each state of matter.

   • Identify ways to measure forms of matter.

Explore Online

 EVIDENCE NOTEBOOK Use the information you've collected in your Evidence Notebook to help you cover each point above.

_____

_____

_____

_____

_____

_____

Checkpoints

2. Select the correct words from the word bank to complete each sentence.

solid	liquid	gas	fast
slow	low	high	

A _____ is a state of matter that has a definite shape. The speed of its

particles is very _____ related to other states of matter. These particles have

very _____ energy due to their speed.

97

3. Draw lines to match the tools in the right-hand column with the things they measure.

volume	balance
length	graduated cylinder
weight	metric ruler

4. Label each illustration with the term that describes the state of matter: solid, liquid, or gas.

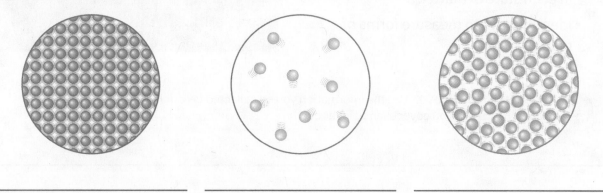

_____   _____   _____

5. Select the appropriate term to complete the sentence.

| displacement   length × height × weight   a balance |

In order to measure the volume of an irregularly shaped object, the best

method to use is _____.

6. Choose the correct words from the word bank to complete each sentence.

| solid   liquid   gas   weight |
| volume   matter   balance   displacement |

The three states of _____ are _____, _____,

and _____.

One way to measure the _____ of a solid is by _____ of water.

A _____ measures the _____ of a solid.

Lesson Roundup

A. Matter is anything that takes up space. Which of these are considered types of matter? Circle all that apply.

1. a feeling of happiness
2. a thought
3. a chicken laying an egg
4. a container filled with milk
5. five minutes passing by
6. bowling pins set up on an alley

B. Choose the correct words from the word bank to complete the sentence.

| particles | large | gases | small |

All matter is made of _____. Most are too _____ to see

without a very strong microscope.

C. How do you calculate the volume of a solid? What is the volume of these solid objects? Complete the table.

	Length	Width	Height	Volume
Object 1	10	5	10	
Object 2	12	3	20	
Object 3	20	10	30	

D. Match the types of measuring tools with the properties they can measure.

| balance | scale | displacement | metric ruler |
| ruler | meter stick | length × width × height | |

Length	Weight	Volume

What Are Properties of Matter?

This salt water aquarium contains different types of matter, living and nonliving, in different states: solids, liquids, and gases.

By the end of this lesson . . .
you will be able to describe and recognize properties of matter and how those properties are affected by different factors.

Matter does not always behave as expected. Look at this substance. Sometimes it behaves like a solid, but when a magnet is near it behaves like a liquid.

1. How would you describe this substance to a friend? What sort of properties would you say it has?

Tip

Learn more about how animals obtain and use energy and matter in How Do Matter and Energy Move Through Ecosystems?

_____

_____

_____

_____

_____

_____

_____

_____

_____

 EVIDENCE NOTEBOOK Look for this icon to help you gather evidence to answer the question above.

What Affects the Rate of Dissolving?

Objective

Do all things dissolve at the same rate? Imagine you are making lemonade on a hot summer day. When you mix the sugar and water and begin to stir, the items mix together. Now, what would happen if you did this same thing on a cold winter day? Would the mixing happen at the same speed? Sometimes by changing certain things, the mixing can go faster or slower.

Collaborate to investigate three different variables. You will see how the type of salt, the temperature of the water, and the rate of stirring impact how fast salt dissolves in water. The ability to dissolve is a property of matter. Knowing how fast or slow something will dissolve helps to identify what substance you have.

Materials

- safety goggles
- lab apron
- 5 spoons for stirring
- 3 clear 100-mL containers
- measuring spoon
- measuring cups
- stopwatch
- room temperature water
- table salt
- coarse salt
- cold tap water
- warm tap water

Objective

What question will you investigate to meet this objective?

_____

_____

_____

_____

Procedure

STEP 1 For each step of the experiment, use a stopwatch to time how long it takes the salt to dissolve. Stop timing if the salt has not completely dissolved after two minutes. Be sure to empty and rinse the containers between each test. Make sure to wear goggles and an apron to protect your clothes, eyes, and skin.

STEP 2 Add 50 mL of room-temperature water to each of the three containers. Add a level tablespoon of table salt to each of the three containers. DO NOT STIR the first container. Stir the second container at a medium speed and the third container at faster speed. Record the time it takes for the salt in each cup to dissolve in the table.

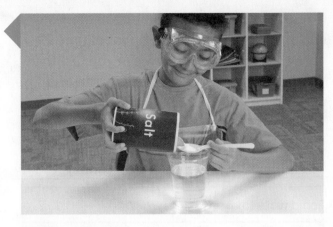

Why did you not stir one of the containers? What purpose does that container serve?

_____

_____

_____

_____

_____

Time It Takes to Dissolve

Treatment	Time (seconds)
no stirring	
stirring slowly	
stirring quickly	

STEP 3 Does the particle size of salt make a difference in the amount of time it takes to dissolve? How can you test the difference between table salt and coarse salt? Make a plan and test it out!

When testing the difference in particle size, what factors did you keep the same between both samples? Why?

_____

_____

_____

_____

_____

Time It Takes to Dissolve

Treatment	Time (seconds)
coarse salt	
table salt	

STEP 4 Does the temperature of the water make a difference in the amount of time it takes salt to dissolve? How can you test the temperature difference? Make a plan and test it out!

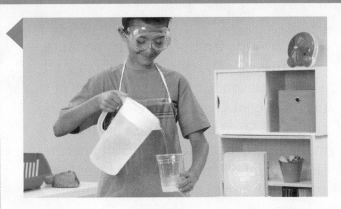

Time It Takes to Dissolve	
Treatment	Time (seconds)
cold water	
warm water	

Look at your data. What would happen if the water were boiling?

_____

_____

Analyze Your Results

STEP 5 Which type of stirring caused the salt to dissolve the fastest?

_____

_____

_____

_____

STEP 6 Select one of the factors you tested. Graph your data on the graph.

Compare your graph with another group's graph. What does your graph say about the rate of dissolving?

_____

_____

_____

_____

STEP 7 Which type of salt dissolved at a faster rate?

_____

STEP 8 Which temperature of water caused the salt to dissolve the fastest?

_____

STEP 9 How did the salt in the water that was not stirred compare to the salt in the water that was stirred quickly or slowly?

_____

STEP 10 What questions do you have about how certain substances dissolve?

_____

_____

_____

Draw Conclusions

STEP 11 Why do you think that stirring the salt at a high rate of speed caused it to dissolve faster than the slower rate?

_____

_____

_____

STEP 12 Why do you think the coarse salt took a different amount of time than the table salt to dissolve?

_____

_____

_____

STEP 13 Make a claim based on your investigation and support it with evidence.

_____

_____

_____

105

So Many Properties

Properties Describe Matter

All matter has properties. Some of the easiest properties to identify are the color, shape, and size of an object. These are called **physical properties**—characteristics of matter that you can observe or measure directly. No matter what terms you use, being able to describe an object using its properties is very important in science.

2. What properties describe this hat? Think about its color, size, and shape. Use words that really tell about the hat.

_____

_____

_____

_____

Identifying Properties

3. Look at the pictures, and then complete the table below. Choose your own property to describe for the last column.

	Color	Shape	
Ducks			
Flower			

High-Priority Properties

Finding common properties or characteristics among objects can help scientists organize and classify them. But what happens when some properties match but others do not?

Property Categories

4. Sort the different objects according to shared properties by choosing a property, and writing the name of each object in the columns.

Color		

5. How did you sort the objects?

_____

_____

_____

Amazing Properties of Matter!

Color and shape are two basic properties of matter. Many other properties help you tell one type of matter from another.

Some properties, like reflectivity and response to magnetic forces, are important to scientists and engineers. An engineer designing a new type of magnetic device would not use wood to build it, because wood does not react to magnetic forces. Remember the substance that was discussed at the beginning of the lesson, which behaves sometimes like a solid and sometimes like a liquid? Response to magnetic forces is the property that causes that strange behavior.

Most rocks are hard. Feathers are soft. Hardness describes how easily something can be bent or dented.

Reflectivity is the ability to reflect light. Smooth objects, like this tea set, tend to be more reflective than objects that are bumpy.

6. Your teacher hands you three objects: a piece of wood, a metal nail, and a rubber band. Using the properties on these two pages, describe how you know what each of the objects is, and how it behaves.

_____

_____

_____

_____

_____

HANDS-ON Apply What You Know

Bridge Building

7. How do physical properties affect the materials you select to build a model of a bridge? Come up with a plan to test different materials. With your teacher's permission, build your model. Which materials worked? Which did not? What physical properties describe the materials that are part of a successful bridge model?

This electromagnet attracts scrap metal for sorting. Response to magnetic forces is a physical property that is very useful at garbage dumps and recycling centers.

How can you bend a long, skinny balloon into all of those other shapes? The balloons are rubber. Rubber is flexible, so it bends easily.

8. Choose the correct words to complete each sentence.

> hardness   flexible   magnets   reflectivity

Some objects that are _____ can bend without breaking. Objects

that are attracted to _____ are usually made of metal. Mirrors and

glass can be easily identified by the property of _____ .

_____ is a property that describes a brick wall.

 EVIDENCE NOTEBOOK Think about how the properties you've learned about so far—color, size, shape, hardness, and reflectivity—would be good or not so good for identifying types of matter. Enter your answers in your Evidence Notebook.

Conductivity (Thermal and Electrical)

You have already learned about several different properties that matter can have. Another one to add the list is conductivity—the ability to transfer heat or electricity. Materials that let heat or electricity travel through them easily are conductive. Most things that are conductors are made of metal, although other materials can be conductive as well.

Materials that do not conduct heat or electricity or are called insulators. Insulation is often made of cloth, plastic, or rubber. In fact, have you ever noticed what covers the electric power cords of electric devices? The wires inside are covered with plastic to keep the electricity and heat from flowing out and starting a fire.

9. Why would holding up a metal umbrella during a lightning storm be a bad idea?

_____

_____

_____

Using a metal spoon to stir the pot could result in a burn to your hands because metal conducts heat from boiling water.

Using a spoon with a nylon handle is a much better idea. Nylon does not conduct heat as well as metal.

10. The spoon in the left-hand pot of boiling water is made of

_____. It is a good _____ of heat and electricity.

Just looking at something isn't a good way to determine its conductivity. Objects may be very polished so they look like metal but are actually made of plastic. The best way to test for conductivity is to see if the object heats up, just like the spoons in the previous photos.

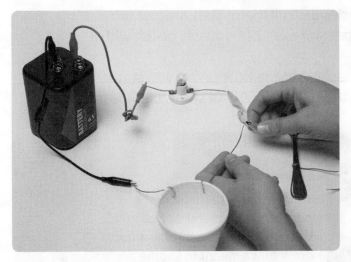

Explore Online

Many things conduct electricity and heat, while others do not. Which conductors do you think will make the light go on? Most objects made of metal are good conductors. Objects made of plastic or wood are not. Objects made of other materials may or may not conduct electricity or heat.

HANDS-ON Apply What You Know

Conducting Conductors

11. You can make your own circuits to test different materials for conductivity. Your teacher will provide you with a light bulb in a holder, some copper wire, a AA battery, and a few materials to test. You will need to put on safety goggles and heat-resistant gloves.

    Attach one end of a wire to the light bulb. Attach the other end of that wire to one side of the battery. Attach one end of the other wire to the light bulb. Place the material to be tested between the other end of this second wire and the other side of the battery. If the bulb lights up, what can you say about the material?

Language SmArts
Researching Insulators and Conductors

12. Research conductors and insulators to compare their properties. Determine the traits of good conductors and good insulators. Describe how they differ.

Dissolving and Evaporating

Matter has so many different properties that it is hard to keep track. Another property of matter you should consider is solubility, which is the ability of one substance to dissolve in another. When something dissolves, it may look like one substance has disappeared, but those particles are still there! They are just too small to be seen. If you let salt water evaporate, for example, you will be left with a pile of salt.

Think back to the activity you did with the salt and the water. After you stirred the water with the salt in it, was the salt still there? You could not see it, but it was still in the water. It had dissolved.

You may have seen a sodium bicarbonate tablet dropped in water to produce a bubbly antacid drink that's meant to soothe an upset stomach. The solid seems to disappear as it reacts with water and produces bubbles. This means sodium bicarbonate is soluble in water.

These salt deposits are the product of salt water evaporating.

Do the Math

Interpret a Graph

13. Bodhi investigated how temperature and volume affect how long it takes liquid to evaporate in class. Identify the patterns he discovered and graphed.

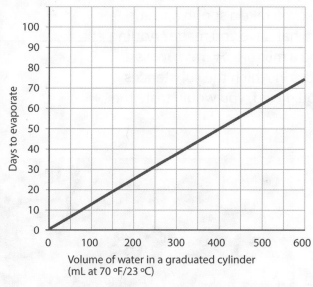

Volume of water in a graduated cylinder
(mL at 70 °F/23 °C)

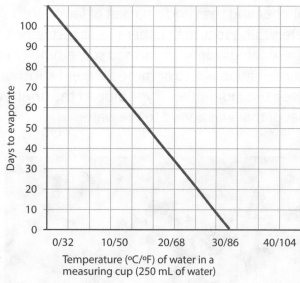

Temperature (°C/°F) of water in a
measuring cup (250 mL of water)

14. Describe how long it takes different volumes of water to evaporate.

_____

_____

15. Describe how long it takes different temperatures of water to evaporate.

_____

_____

 EVIDENCE NOTEBOOK What evidence would you need to determine if something shows the properties of solubility, flexibility, and magnetism? Enter your answer in your Evidence Notebook.

Putting It Together

16. List four properties of matter that can be used to determine and describe an object.

_____

_____

Mixtures and Solutions

What Is It?

Imagine you are making a drink from a mix. You add water to a pitcher and then add a packet of flavor crystals. You take a spoon and stir everything together. Other than a tasty drink, what have you made? Adding these things together formed something called a mixture. A **mixture** is a combination of two or more different substances in which the substances keep their identities. If you sipped the drink you mixed, you would taste the flavor that was added to the water.

This salad is a great example of a mixture. Even though they are mixed together, you can still see all of the different vegetables.

Some types of orange juice are made by mixing water with a smaller volume of concentrated orange juice.

In a mixture, each part keeps its own properties. Have you ever accidentally swallowed some ocean water? If so, then you have tasted a mixture—water and salt. Mixtures can often be separated. If you leave a dish of ocean water out in the sun, the water evaporates, and a small pile of salt remains.

17. Name a mixture you may find at a meal.

_____

_____

_____

_____

Have you ever been to the beach? Take a close look at the sand under your feet. If you look closely, you can see that it has many different colors and sizes of particles. You may also be able to see tiny parts of seashells.

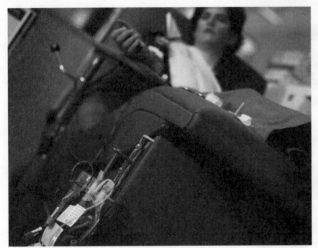

You have a mixture inside of you. Your blood is a mixture made of water and different types of cells. Some of these cells carry oxygen. Others fight off infections. Other parts of blood help to stop bleeding if you get a cut.

Go outside, and take a close look at a street. It is another type of mixture. Asphalt is made of many different sizes of particles. A heavy machine blends and presses these particles and a type of oil together to make a road.

18. Choose the correct words to complete each sentence.

mixture	physical trait	behavior	properties
separated	shrunk	salad	bread

When particles are blended together, they form a substance

called a _____. When this happens, each particle

keeps its own _____. One thing that is special here

is that the particles can always be _____. A good

example of a mixture is _____.

What Is a Solution?

Some mixtures are obvious, such as a salad. Other mixtures, such as ocean water, are so well blended that it's hard to know they contain more than one thing. A mixture that has the same composition throughout because its parts are mixed evenly is called a **solution**.

Think of lemonade, ocean water, or orange juice. Can you see the different parts that make up these liquids? Probably not. That is because the solids, such as the sugar in lemonade, have dissolved into the water. The particles are too small to be seen. You can taste them, but you cannot see them. How could you collect the solids? As with salt water, you could let lemonade sit out in the sun until the water evaporates. You would be left with a pile of lemony sugar.

Ocean water is a great example of a solution. What kinds of things can be found in it? Ocean water has a lot of dissolved salt in it, which is why you cannot drink it. All of the organisms living in the ocean have ways to drink or absorb water but avoid too much salt. Ocean water also has small amounts of other substances, including calcium and potassium.

Adding food coloring to water is a good way to observe how a solution is made. When the coloring is first dropped in, you can still see it distinctly. But after stirring it, the coloring is spread out evenly in the water. You cannot see where the coloring starts or the water ends.

When you think of solutions, you probably think of liquids. However, solutions can also be mixtures of gases. The solution of gases that you are probably most familiar with is air. Nitrogen, carbon dioxide, oxygen, and other gases all mix together to form the mixture you breathe.

This hang glider flies through the air. Air is a mixture of different gases.

Do you help with the dishes after dinner? The soap you use is a solution. It has several different things mixed together that help get the dishes clean.

19. Fill in the blank with the best term.

A taco is a good example of a _____ because all of its parts

can be seen.

Lemonade is an example of a _____ because its parts are so

well mixed that they can't be easily seen or separated.

 EVIDENCE NOTEBOOK How would you know if something is a solution or just a mixture? Enter your answers in your Evidence Notebook.

Separating Mixtures

You now know that mixtures are combinations of matter where each part keeps its own properties. Think back to the salad you saw earlier. What kinds of things did you see in this mixture? Now, imagine you want to remove all of the carrots and cucumbers from the rest of the salad.

Sometimes solutions need to be separated. There are several different ways this can be done. Some of these ways involve the use of advanced equipment, while others use very simple methods.

Mixed and Sorted

20. Identify how the two mixtures below were sorted.

 **Explore Online**

The salad is made of different vegetables. How can these ingredients be separated?

_____

_____

_____

_____

_____

_____

_____

The messy workbench gets sorted into metal and nonmetal piles. How?

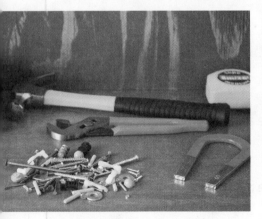 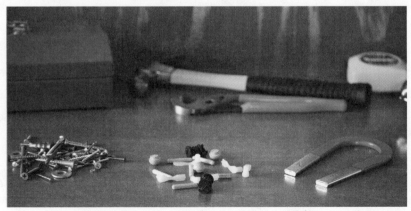

_____

_____

When particles are mixed so well together that other separation methods don't work, sometimes scientists have to resort to very advanced techniques. DNA is the part of your cells that carries the code for all of your traits. Because there is so much of it inside each cell, scientists need to separate different segments to be able to "read" it. They do this by sending electricity through a gel that has segments of DNA at one end. The different-sized segments travel different lengths along the shell, creating a DNA "fingerprint." You can model this method of separating a mixture in the Hands-On Activity.

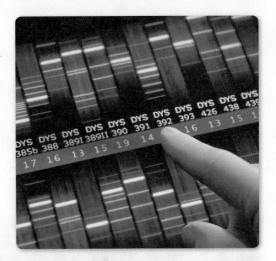

HANDS-ON Apply What You Know

Colors on the Move

21. You are now going to use your knowledge of mixtures and solutions to separate a mixture. Paper chromatography is a way scientists separate different pigments. Inks and dyes are often made from different pigments mixed together. Your job will be to separate them.

Using scissors, cut several strips of the filter paper. Using the black marker, draw a large dot about one half-inch up from the bottom. Do the same thing using the other pens on the other strips of filter paper. Tape the strip to a pencil so that it will hang down into the cup. Pour water into the cup until it barely touches the bottom of the strip. Let the strip hang until the color has traveled most of the way up the filter paper strip.

Materials
- scissors
- filter paper
- black marker and non-primary color pens
- 5 clear 100-mL beakers
- tape
- several pencils
- water
- ruler

22. How would you go about separating the materials found in an unorganized desk drawer? After you have written your response, go carry out your plan.

_____

_____

_____

_____

_____

Engineer It!
Alloys

You might think metals are strong, but most metals are really quite weak. It is only when they are mixed with other metals that they get their strength. When metals are mixed together, they form a new material called an *alloy*. Scientists and engineers use alloys when they design and build buildings. Alloys are thought of as a solution of metals. Stainless steel, pewter, and 18-carat gold are all examples of alloys.

In order to create an alloy, the metals often have to be melted down. To do this, it takes a very hot temperature. Once the metals are in liquid form, they are mixed together. When they cool, a new, stronger metal is formed.

If the metal used in a building were not strong, the structure would topple over in the first wind storm. Steel is one of the strongest alloys used for buildings. It is a mixture of iron, carbon, and other substances.

Language SmArts
A Solution of Metals

23. The engines of airplanes are made of materials called superalloys. Do some research on superalloys and where and why they are commonly used.

_____

_____

_____

Putting It Together

24. What is a mixture, and why are solutions considered the "best mixed" ones?

_____

_____

_____

_____

Discover More

Check out this path... or go online to choose one of these other paths.

People in Science & Engineering

- **Healthy Mixtures**
- **Mineral Hardness Scale**

Shirley Ann Jackson and Anthony Atala

▷ **Explore Online**

Two modern scientists have spent their careers studying the properties of matter. Dr. Shirley Ann Jackson is a physicist who studies how particles move to different places. She has done research on tiny devices called semiconductors, which are used in electronics.

Dr. Anthony Atala is a physician and medical researcher who is pioneering the use of 3D printers in regenerative medicine—making tissues and even organs that can be tailored to specific patients who are suffering from organ failure or have been injured.

Dr. Shirley Ann Jackson is the president of Rensselaer Polytechnic Institute in New York. She is the first African American woman to receive a doctoral degree from the Massachusetts Institute of Technology. Her interests include the properties of semiconductors and how they work in lasers, optics, and other machines.

Dr. Shirley Ann Jackson

Semiconductors are at the center of just about anything that has a computer chip. They are often made of a material called silicon. One of their properties is that they work somewhere between a conductor and an insulator. This property makes them very useful in electronic devices.

121

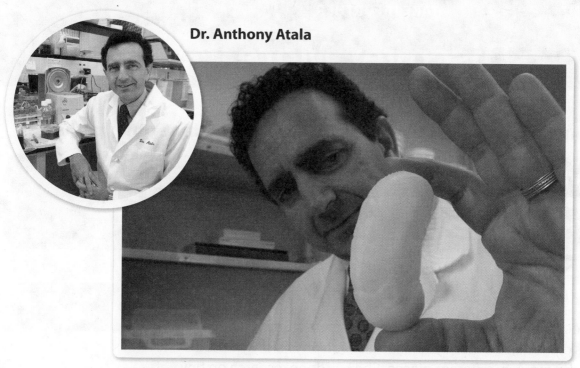

Dr. Anthony Atala

At the Wake Forest Institute for Regenerative Medicine, Dr. Atala and his team have developed a method of "printing" human tissues.

Dr. Anthony Atala was born in Peru and raised in Florida. He earned his M.D. from the University of Louisville and is now the director of the Wake Forest Institute for Regenerative Medicine. One of the projects Dr. Atala and his colleagues are working on is bioprinting, which combines the technology of 3D printing with medicine.

A 3D printer uses plastic or wax to create an object from a computer-drawn design. Dr. Atala's printers are a little different—they print living cells onto a supporting structure that can then be transplanted into a human.

Dr. Atala hopes this technology will one day eliminate the long waits that many ill patients have to endure before receiving vital organs such as kidneys and bladders. Replacement tissues and organs could also be grown and printed to treat wounded soldiers and others who have lost tissue or have damaged organs.

25. How can knowing the properties of matter lead to new technologies?

_____

_____

_____

_____

_____

Lesson Check

Name _____

Can You Explain It?

1. Use what you have learned about properties of matter to describe the properties of this substance and explain how it is alike and different from other matter. Be sure to do the following:

   • Describe the properties of the substance.

   • Explain if the substance is a solid or a liquid.

   • Identify how the substance has flexibility but is also solid in some ways.

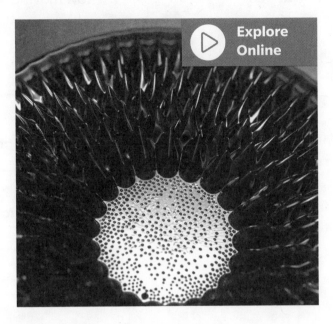

Explore Online ▷

📋 **EVIDENCE NOTEBOOK** Use the information you've collected in your Evidence Notebook to help you cover each point.

_____

_____

_____

_____

_____

_____

_____

_____

Checkpoints

2. Why is a vegetable salad considered a mixture?

   a. The particles are very small.

   b. The vegetables can be put together easily.

   c. Each part keeps its own identity.

   d. All of the colors and flavors fit well together.

3. Suppose you were asked to identify the properties of most fire trucks. Select all the terms that you could use.

a. red

b. purple

c. large

d. round

e. long

f. slow moving

g. very speedy

h. loud

i. soft

4. Match the objects in the word bank to the property that it best demonstrates.

rubber band	bungee cord	brick
feather	iron bar	metal fork

Elasticity	hardness	conductivity

5. You have a shallow container filled with ocean water. What could you do to separate the salt from the ocean water?

a. Add additional water to the container.

b. Let it stand in the sun for a while.

c. Take some water out of the container.

d. Decrease the temperature of the water.

6. Choose the correct words to complete each sentence.

dissolve	evaporate	slowly	quickly
increase	decrease	temperature	conductivity

When trying to get salt to _____ in water, it is best to stir

it _____. If you wanted to get the salt into solution faster,

you could _____ the _____ of the water.

Lesson Roundup

A. Suppose you were asked to design a machine that would be made of materials that will best conduct electricity. Select those that would be useful to you.

1. plastic   **3.** aluminum   **5.** rubber   **7.** flannel

2. wood   **4.** gold   **6.** silk

B. Choose the correct words to complete each sentence.

red	purple	giraffe	button	paper clip
grasshopper	an ice cube	an ice cream cone	a shoebox	

You have a ripe apple and a picture of a stop sign. Both of these objects are

_____ in color, so they can be sorted this way. Two things that can

be sorted by similar size are a _____ and a _____

When sorting by shape, _____ and _____ would be in

the same category.

C. A scientist has a special container of ocean water. She wants to keep it so she can study it further. Her lab gets a lot of sunlight every day. What can she do to keep the ocean water from turning into just a pile of salt?

1. cover the container to prevent evaporation

2. increase the temperature of the container

3. separate the water into different containers

4. add more plain water to the container

D. A solution is a special type of mixture. An alloy is a special type of solution. Select all of the properties of an alloy.

1. can be easily separated   **5.** high flexibility

2. very strong   **6.** conductivity

3. made of metals   **7.** insulator

4. high elasticity

How Does Matter Change?

In this location, water exists in three different states: liquid, solid, and gas.

By the end of this lesson . . .
you'll be able to identify different changes that can happen to matter.

Can You Explain It?

Explore Online

Matter is not always what it seems. In this experiment, two liquids are added together. When they interact, they form a solid. How is this possible?

1. How could a solid result from the mixing of two liquids?

_____

_____

_____

_____

_____

_____

Tip

Review what it means for something to be a liquid or solid in What Are Properties of Matter?

 EVIDENCE NOTEBOOK Look for this icon to help you gather evidence to answer the question above.

Physical Changes

Ch, Ch, Ch, Changes

One of the ways matter can be changed is in how it looks. It can be scribbed with pencil and change color. It can be cut into many pieces. It can be bent into a different shape. The matter itself is still the same. This type of change is called a **physical change.** The key to a physical change is that nothing new is made.

There's a stack of paper. Some of it gets folded into this crane. Is it still paper? Yes! Folding it is just changing its shape. This is a great example of a physical change.

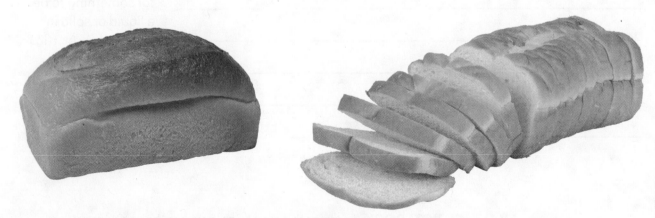

To make a sandwich, you have to cut slices from this loaf of bread. Once the slices are in the sandwich, you have made a new substance, right? Wrong! The slices of bread are made of exactly the same stuff as the unsliced bread.

Another example of a physical change happens when you mix things together. Imagine you have a bag of blue beads and a bag of red beads. Then you put them together into the same bag and shake it up. What happens? The beads mix with each other. Can you still see the different colors? Yes! This is because you have not created anything new. The physical change is just the mixing of the beads.

This can is made of steel. It is used to hold soup or vegetables. What happens to the can after it gets crushed? Is the can still made of steel? Sure! All you have done by crushing it is change its shape. It is still the same kind of matter.

2. Choose the correct words for each sentence.

color	location	makeup	shape	cutting
burning	matter	temperature	flammability	size

Physical changes happen when matter changes _____,

_____, or _____.

An example of this type of change would be _____

a piece of wood. In this type of change, no new _____

is created.

 EVIDENCE NOTEBOOK What evidence have you found that a physical change has occurred? Enter your answers in your Evidence Notebook.

Physical Changes Up Close: Melting and Freezing

Remember that matter can exist in different states. Solids, liquids, and gases are the three most common states of matter on Earth. These states are also important to know when thinking about physical changes. Changing from one state to another is an example of a physical change. The thing to keep in mind when looking at these changes of state is that no new matter is made. The matter you started with is still there, just in a different form.

Have you ever put orange juice into the freezer? It becomes a solid. To make orange juice ice pops, pour orange juice into an ice cube tray. Then cover the top with plastic wrap. Punch a toothpick into each chamber and then put it in the freezer. In a couple of hours, you will have a treat! Physical changes in action!

3. How does the orange juice compare in each of its different states?

_____

_____

_____

_____

_____

Freezing and melting are two common physical changes. When you freeze a liquid, its particles slow down because they have less energy. Remember that the particles in solids vibrate in fixed positions. Freezing a liquid changes it into a solid. When you take that solid out of the freezer and warm it up, it is called melting. When the temperature is warmer, the particles gain energy and start to move faster. When they gain enough energy, they break loose and slide past one another. This changes the solid into a liquid.

Do the Math

Explaining Patterns in Melting

4. Substances change their state at different temperatures. The substances at right all change from solids to liquids with different amounts of energy.

   Which substance has the highest melting point? Which substance has the lowest melting point? Would the substance that melts at the lowest melting point also melt at the highest melting point? Explain your answer.

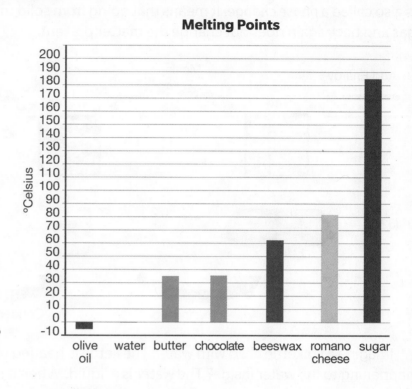

Melting Points

°Celsius

olive oil, water, butter, chocolate, beeswax, romano cheese, sugar

_____

_____

_____

_____

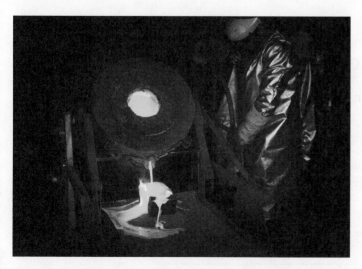

The **melting point** is the temperature at which a solid changes to a liquid. This metal, which was once a solid, is now a liquid. Different metals have different melting points. For example, tin has a lower melting point than iron.

5. Enter *freezing* or *boiling* to complete the sentence.

   To turn this liquid back into a solid, it needs to be at its _____ point.

Phase In, Phase Out

Changing the state of matter is an example of a physical change. This is also called a *phase change.* It means that going from solid to liquid to gas and back again does not change the matter present.

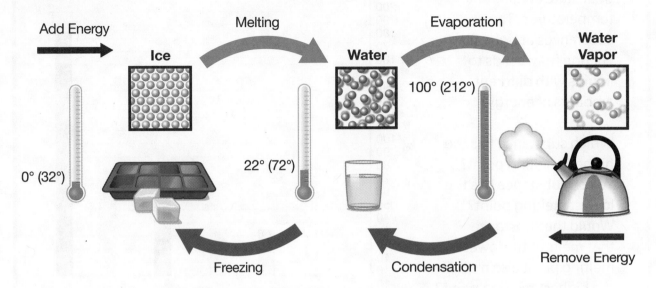

Imagine a teakettle filled with water. The kettle is heating up. What is happening to the water inside? The water is a liquid. When it reaches its boiling point, it will turn into a gas. The **boiling point** is the temperature at which matter changes from a liquid to a gas. As the gas tries to escape from the kettle, it whistles (remember that gas particles move very fast). After the kettle is removed from the heat, it will start to cool. This changes the gas back into a liquid. If that liquid water is then placed into the freezer, it will cool more. It will then become a solid. All this time, physical changes have been happening. Nothing new has been made.

Language SmArts
Making Rice in the Kitchen

6. What changes happen to water when making rice?

_____

_____

_____

_____

_____

_____

_____

> **Tip**
>
> The English Language Arts Handbook can provide help with understanding how to determine sequence of events.

Which Will React?

Objective

Collaborate to identify substances. The ingredients in a kitchen have lost their labels. How can you tell the cornstarch, cream of tartar, and baking soda apart? Just by looking at them you can't tell. But by observing if a mystery substance undergoes a physical or chemical change you can often determine what it is.

What question will you investigate to meet this objective?

_____

_____

_____

_____

Materials

- safety goggles
- apron
- 3 droppers
- 3 plastic spoons
- 9 test tubes
- test tube holder
- dry ingredient 1
- dry ingredient 2
- dry ingredient 3
- iodine solution
- vinegar
- water
- labels and pen
- test tube brush
- soap

Procedure

STEP 1 A 5th grade student has three containers, each with white powders in them. She is confused as to what they are. She needs to figure out which is baking soda, cornstarch, and cream of tartar, but they look the same and have no labels.

STEP 2 Label three water test tubes "A," "B," and "C." Prepare test tubes the same way for the vinegar and iodine. Carefully place each test tube in the test tube holder.

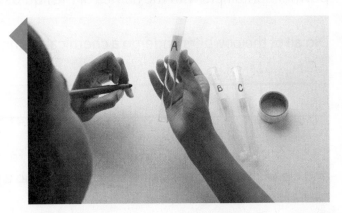

133

STEP 3 Add a tiny spoonful of powder 1 to the first set of test tubes water "A," vinegar "A," and iodine "A."

STEP 4 Repeat Step 3 with powder 2 and powder 3, making sure that powder 2 only goes in test tubes with a *B*, and powder 3 only goes in test tubes with a *C*.

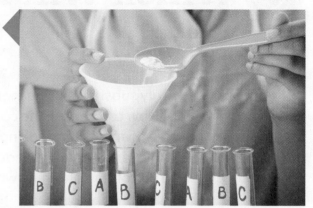

STEP 5 Using a dropper, add three drops of water to all three water test tubes. Record your results in the table.

STEP 6 Use a different dropper and add three drops of vinegar to all three vinegar test tubes. Record your results in the table.

STEP 7 Now use a third dropper to add three drops of iodine to all three iodine test tubes. Record your results in the table.

Do you think three drops is enough to see a reaction? Would you get the same result with only two drops?

DATA TABLE: Reactions			
	A (Powder 1)	B (Powder 2)	C (Powder 3)
Water			
Vinegar			
Iodine			

STEP 8 Analyze your results on the table. Using your observations, label the powder containers with the names of the liquids that reacted with each one.

Did all of the powders undergo a chemical change?

_____

_____

STEP 9 Once you are done recording all the reactions, keep your safety gear on and clean the test tubes using soap, water, and a test tube brush.

Analyze Your Results

STEP 10 Baking soda will react with vinegar to produce a gas. Cornstarch will mix with iodine and change color. Cream of tartar will not react with water, vinegar, or iodine. Using this information, complete the table below to identify each mystery ingredient.

Powder #1	Powder #2	Powder #3

STEP 11 What effect did the vinegar have on the baking soda? Did any of the other tests show the same effect as the baking soda and vinegar?

_____

_____

_____

STEP 12 What reaction did you see with the cornstarch and iodine solution? Did any others react in the same way?

_____

_____

_____

STEP 13 What was the purpose of testing the cream of tartar?

_____

_____

_____

Draw Conclusions

STEP 14 Make a claim about which types of changes took place in this investigation. Support your answer with evidence.

_____

_____

_____

_____

Chemical Changes

Before and After Are Different

Another type of change that can occur is a chemical change. During a **chemical change,** new matter is formed. There may be a new product (such as a *precipitate,* the solid material that forms at the bottom of a tube) or a gas. Or you may observe an increase in temperature. The key thing is that the original matter has changed for good.

Burning things is a great example of a chemical change. When something burns, energy is released in the form of heat. The burning substance changes into something new as heat is released. Think of the pile of ashes that remains after a campfire has burned out. You cannot make the ashes change back into wood.

 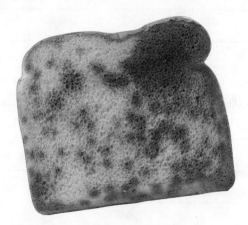

What happens when you leave food out on the counter or in the refrigerator for a long time? It "goes bad," or rots. The chemical makeup of the food changes.

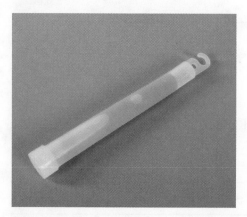 

Glow sticks have chemicals inside of them. When these chemicals come together, they start to glow. Can you ever separate those chemicals? No. This is because a chemical change has happened. Once the reaction is over, the light will die out.

If you cook eggs, then you have seen the result of a chemical change. Once you crack the egg into the hot pan, the heat starts to change it. The liquid part of the egg now becomes more solid and changes color. The smell of the cooking egg is another sign that a chemical change is taking place. Once cooked, there's no way to put the egg back into its original state.

7. Categorize the following changes or products as evidence of chemical or physical change.

| strong odor | temperature change | precipitate |
| breaking in half | bending | painting |

Chemical change	Physical change

 HANDS-ON Apply What You Know

Seeing Chemical Changes

8. Your teacher will provide you with Epsom salts and ammonia. Use a balance to measure out 2 g of the Epsom salts and place them into a beaker. Then use a graduated cylinder to measure out 10 mL of ammonia (safety note*—be sure to wear safety goggles, do not touch the ammonia, and do the activity in a well-ventilated area). Add the ammonia to the beaker of Epsom salts, and set a timer for 5 hours. Monitor the beaker regularly, and record your observations.

 EVIDENCE NOTEBOOK What happened to the Epsom salts immediately after you added the ammonia? What happened to the Epsom salts over time? What evidence did you collect that showed a chemical change happened? How is this different from a physical change? Record your answers and evidence in your Evidence Notebook.

Chemical Changes Up Close: Rusting and Rotting

Have you ever seen a rusty metal can? Rusting is another example of a chemical change. If metals are not protected and they get wet, they may start to rust. The water causes the metal to develop a reddish-brown color. Over time, the spot where the rust forms will "eat away" at the can. This will form a hole. The rust will spread, and the entire metal can will fall apart.

9. Describe the appearance of the car and the environment it's in.

_____

_____

_____

_____

_____

10. How has the scene changed?

_____

_____

_____

_____

11. How about now?

_____

_____

_____

_____

Engineer It!
Electroplating

Did you know electricity is able to cause chemical changes? Engineers use electricity to cause chemical changes in metals in a process called *electroplating*. During this process, an electric current produces chemical changes that result in one metal being coated with a thin layer of another metal. Electroplating is used to improve the durability and appearance of metal objects. The coating prevents unwanted physical and chemical changes from occurring in the metal.

▷ Explore Online

An electric change is applied to both metals, causing them to join. The coated metal may have a different color or other new properties.

Electroplating was used to develop gold-plated visors for astronauts to protect them against the unfiltered rays of the sun.

Electroplating changes the surface of metal objects. This gives the metal different properties. Iron nails, nuts, and bolts are commonly plated with zinc to keep them from rusting. Attractive yet more affordable jewelry is made by placing silver or gold plating on a less expensive metal. Electroplating is also used to give electronic and computer parts more desirable physical properties and to make them last longer. Electroplating is even used to make coins. The pennies we use today consist of a solid zinc core covered with a thin plating of copper.

12. Why is electroplating an example of a chemical change?

_____

_____

_____

_____

_____

Changes at Home: Cooking Science

Did you know that there are all kinds of chemical changes that happen in the kitchen? Remember that a chemical change results in something new being produced and the original materials are used up, or changed into something else. What types of things happen in the kitchen that result in new things being made? Do you like bananas? Bananas change from green to yellow as they ripen. Eventually they turn brown and get mushy. Ripening is a chemical change.

Home-Cooked Chemistry

This family is cooking a meal. They have washed their hands and gathered all the things they need. It also looks like they are going to make something with graham crackers and marshmallows. On the stovetop is a sauté pan with colorful vegetables in it. The father is stirring it while a loaf of bread is baking in the oven.

13. What kinds of energy are causing chemical changes as the meal is prepared?

_____

_____

_____

Baking bread in the oven is a chemical change. What gets put into the dough for bread? Flour, sugar, yeast, and eggs are blended together. After the bread is baked, it has undergone a chemical change to form something new.

Stir-frying vegetables on the stovetop is another example of a chemical change. As they cook, the vegetables become sweeter and slightly brown, due to the heat.

What do you get when you take graham crackers, chocolate, and marshmallows and add a chemical change? S'mores! The roasted marshmallow and chocolate melt together and stick to the cracker. Who knew a chemical change could taste so good?

Composting is another example of a chemical change. The food scraps that go into a compost pile break down over time. The scraps will eventually turn into a nutrient-rich soil. The unpleasant smell of the compost pile is another clue that chemical changes are taking place.

14. Choose words that correctly complete the sentences.

| chemical | physical | mix | separate | always | never |

Baking bread is an example of a _____ change. The ingredients of

the bread _____ to form a new substance. The original ingredients

can _____ be separated.

EVIDENCE NOTEBOOK What types of things happen in the kitchen that are chemical changes? How do you know these are chemical changes? Enter your answers in your Evidence Notebook.

What Kind of Change Is It?

Did you know that the same substance can undergo both physical and chemical changes? Remember that during physical changes, the substance stays the same but changes a property. During chemical changes, new substances are formed .

This pile of wood used to be a tall tree. The person chopped it into smaller pieces. Is it still the same wood? Yes! This would be a physical change.

Now that same wood is placed into a fireplace. It starts to burn. After it is all burned up, what will be left? Will you still have the same wood? No. The wood will be changed into ash.

This loaf of bread is perfect for a sandwich. Using cookie cutters lets you make it into fun shapes. This is a physical change because the bread is just a different shape.

Putting bread in the toaster will make it warm and golden brown. What kind of change is this? Can the original bread ever come back? No. This is a chemical change.

Putting it Together

15. Describe one type of cooking that involves both physical and chemical changes.

_____

_____

_____

_____

_____

Conservation of Matter

Physical Changes

During a physical change, the amount of matter in the object stays the same. This happens because no new matter is being formed. When you cut a piece of paper in half, you still have the same amount of paper, just in two pieces. The fact that the amount of matter stays the same is called the **conservation of matter.**

Imagine you have a pile of building blocks. You build a tower using all of the blocks. Then you are asked to take apart the tower and build another shape using the same number of blocks. The new shape looks totally different than the tower but still has the exact same number of blocks in it. This is the conservation of matter during a physical change.

An orange is being weighed on a digital scale.

The same orange has been peeled and sectioned. How does its weight compare with that of the entire orange?

These are the materials needed for an activity. The sugar and the water will be added together. What is their combined weight here?

The sugar has been added to the water. What is the weight now? Did it change from before they were added together? This is how the conservation of matter works.

Conservation in a Phase Change

The conservation of matter also applies to phase changes. Remember that changing from a solid to a liquid to a gas are all physical changes. The matter does not change, only the speed of its particles. If you were to melt solid gold to a liquid, you would see that it has the same weight as the solid.

215 g

Here is a block of ice sitting in a beaker. Notice what the scale says. This beaker will be left out at room temperature.

215 g

What does the ice look like now? Here it is partially melted and partially solid. You know this because there is some liquid water in the beaker. What does the scale say the weight is?

215 g

The thermometer shows that the ice (now liquid water) is almost near its boiling point. What does the scale say about the weight of the water?

175 g

The water is now at a full boil. Its temperature has also gone up. What does the scale say now about the weight? It says it is less than before. Why is this? Where did the rest of the water go?

HANDS-ON Apply What You Know

Pull the Wool Over Your Eyes

16. In this activity, you will investigate the conservation of matter during a chemical change.

Your teacher will provide you with the steel wool you need to complete the activity. Begin by wetting the steel wool pad and then calculating its weight. Continue to rewet the pad over several days, recording its weight every time until it starts to rust. Let the pad get rusty for a few days before it turns to dust, and then measure its weight one last time.

17. Choose the correct words. Words can be used more than once.

chemical	physical	increase	decrease	stay the same

Phase changes are considered _____ changes. This means

that no new matter is formed. When changing from solid to liquid form,

the weight of the matter will _____. When changing from

liquid to gas form, the weight will _____. This supports the

conservation of matter.

> **EVIDENCE NOTEBOOK** If two liquids combined to form a solid and liquid, how much matter do you think the new substances would have compared to the amounts of matter in the original substances? Record your answer in your Evidence Notebook.

18. Why does the weight change as the water in the beaker changes state?

_____

_____

_____

_____

Conservation of Matter: Chemical Change

Chemical changes also demonstrate the conservation of matter. Remember that in a chemical change new things are formed. However, if you were to collect this new matter and weigh it, you would see that it has the same weight as the original materials. One needs to be careful here, though. Many times, during chemical changes, some of the matter is lost as gas. Therefore, the final weight of the new matter may appear to be less than the original. For example, the weight of the ashes collected after burning paper will be less than the original because some of the weight is lost as gas.

The total weight of a balloon full of baking soda and a flask of vinegar is shown. Notice the weight on the scale.

Vinegar and baking soda produce a liquid and a gas. When this reaction occurs in a flask sealed with a balloon, the gas produced by the reaction is contained. The total weight is unchanged.

19. What would happen if the reaction between baking soda and vinegar occurred in an open container with no balloon? Would it be easy to show conservation of matter?

_____

_____

_____

Putting It Together

20. How does the conservation of matter relate to phase changes?

_____

_____

_____

_____

Discover More

Check out this path . . . or go online to choose one of these other paths.

People in Science & Engineering

- **Slow Down the Spoil**
- **Acids and Bases**

People in Science: Antoine Lavoisier

Conservation of matter is demonstrated during chemical changes. When new substances are formed, their weight will still be the same as the original materials. When burning something, some of the material becomes a gas, and it escapes, the weight of what remains will be slightly less. But conservation of matter still applies!

Explore Online

Antoine Lavoisier was one of the first to realize that the number of things going into a reaction equals the number of things produced. He was very detail-oriented in his studies and collected a lot of data.

When things are heated, a chemical change is taking place. In order to get things to burn, a gas called oxygen must be present. Here, a chemical called *phosphorus* is undergoing a chemical change in the presence of oxygen.

147

Antoine Lavoisier is known as the father of modern chemistry. He was a French scientist who actually started his career as a lawyer. After law school, he got a job at the Royal Gunpowder and Saltpeter Administration. It was here that he began his chemical studies. He is responsible for what we know about how things burn. He discovered oxygen and determined that it made up a percentage of the air we breathe. He also figured out that in order for things to burn, oxygen must be present.

Lavoisier became very curious about how different chemicals could mix together but still have the same weight. He studied the heating of a chemical called mercury oxide. He found that when this was heated, it lost weight. He figured out how to collect the oxygen that is released from the mercury. It turned out that the weight of the oxygen was exactly the same as the decrease in weight of the mercury oxide. This led him to other experiments that would result in him putting together the law of conservation of matter.

If you could capture or contain the tiny smoke particles and gases from a fire and add their weight to the weight of the ash, it would be equal to the weight of the wood and the oxygen it reacted with.

21. What contributions did Antoine Lavoisier make to the understanding of the conservation of matter?

_____

_____

_____

_____

Lesson Check

Name _____

Can You Explain It?

1. Now that you have learned about how chemical and physical changes differ and how they relate to the conservation of matter, explain the different changes that occur. Be sure to do the following:

   • Explain the differences between chemical and physical changes.

   • Describe how you know which type of change has occurred.

   • Explain how the conservation of matter relates to chemical and physical changes

Explore Online

> **EVIDENCE NOTEBOOK** Use the information you've collected in your Evidence Notebook to help you cover each point.

_____

_____

_____

_____

_____

_____

_____

_____

Checkpoints

Answer the following questions to test your knowledge.

2. Which phrase describes a physical change?

   a. bread baking

   b. the smell produced by rotting trash

   c. crumpling paper

   d. gas bubbles rising after adding chemicals together

3. Choose the correct words to complete the sentences.

phase	liquid	freezing point	melting point	boiling point	gas

When matter changes _____, it is a physical change. To do this,

energy is needed. The temperature at which a solid becomes a liquid is called

the _____. If the temperature keeps going up, the _____

will be reached. The liquid will then turn into a _____.

4. Decide which terms relate to chemical changes and which to
physical changes.

Chemical change	Physical change

precipitate

odor

gas produced

color change

shape change

phase change

5. Select the best answer for the question. You leave a glass of ice outside on a sunny
day. When the ice melts, it turns into water. What does the conservation of matter
state about the weight of that water?

a. It will weigh much more
than the ice.

c. It will weigh slightly more
than the ice.

b. It will weigh less than the ice.

d. It will weigh the same as
the ice.

6. Choose the correct words for each sentence.

freezing	melting	energy	matter

A physical change happens when matter changes its phase. Changing

from a solid to a liquid is called _____. This requires an input of

_____. When a liquid changes back into a solid, _____

is removed. This is called _____.

Lesson Roundup

A. Which of the following would be physical changes? Choose all that apply.

1. folding paper
2. breaking a window
3. baking bread
4. food spoiling
5. building a tower out of blocks
6. boiling water

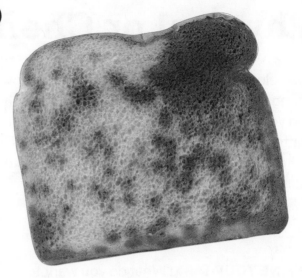

B. Which of the following would be chemical changes? Choose all that apply.

1. bending a metal bar
2. breaking a glass
3. baking brownies
4. fruit getting moldy
5. building a wall out of bricks
6. burning wood in a fireplace

C. Choose the correct words for each sentence.

| burning wood | cutting cardboard | cannot | can |

An example of a chemical change would be _____. When this happens, new matter is formed. This matter _____ be changed back into its original form.

D. Select the correct answer for the question.

What would happen to the amount of matter in a piece of wood if it were cut it into pieces, and then burned?

1. The amount of matter would go up after burning.
2. The amount of matter would go down after cutting into pieces.
3. The amount of matter would increase then decrease when cutting.
4. There would be no change in the amount of matter.

Physical or Chemical?

You belong to a club that puts on science shows for young students. It is your turn to organize a show, and your focus is "The Two Different Ways that Matter Can Change." You are required to develop and demonstrate that topic using three or four examples.

Burning is an example of one type of change that can happen to matter.

DEFINE YOUR TASK: What do you want to accomplish with your demonstration?

_____

_____

_____

Examine the checklist at the end of this activity and be sure that you follow it as you proceed.

RESEARCH: Look up the two ways that matter can change and how to tell the difference. Summarize your research here.

_____

_____

_____

_____

BRAINSTORM: Brainstorm three or four examples of matter changing. Be sure to find examples of both kinds of change.

_____

_____

_____

_____

MAKE A PLAN: Consider the form that your presentation will take.

a. What general concepts do you want to address?

b. In what order should you address those concepts?

c. What materials will you need for your demonstrations, and how will you use those materials?

Present a step-by-step plan here.

_____

_____

_____

_____

_____

EVALUATE: Does your presentation address your topic? What could you add or take away to make it better?

_____

_____

_____

COMMUNICATE: Present your science show to your group.

✓ Checklist

Review your project, and check off each completed item.

_____ Includes definitions and descriptions of the two types of changes in matter

_____ Includes text that orders material in a clear and logical way

_____ Includes an example(s) of physical change in matter and a concise plan to demonstrate it

_____ Includes an example(s) of chemical change in matter and a concise plan to demonstrate it

_____ The science show was presented using the text and examples effectively.

Unit Review

Use this image to answer question 1.

1. Write the correct answer on the line. The matter inside these containers takes up _____ .

2. Place the words in the correct column in the table.

| emotions | clock | helium gas |
| sunlight | magma | sound |

Matter	Not matter

3. Circle the correct answer. What is all matter made of?

   a. plasma

   b. liquid

   c. living things

   d. smaller particles

4. Draw a line from each word in the first column to the state of matter that describes it in the second column.

   nitrogen   solid

   bus

   tea   liquid

   milk

   sidewalk   gas

   hydrogen

Use this image to answer questions 5 and 6.

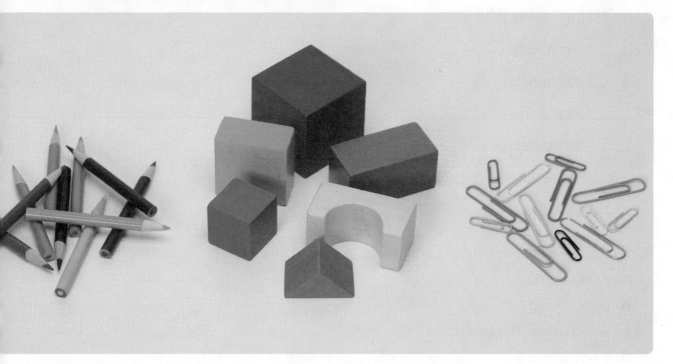

5. Which properties could you use to sort the items in the photo?
   Circle all that apply.

   a. taste

   b. smell

   c. color

   d. shape

   e. luster

   f. size

6. Write the correct word to complete each sentence.

color	size	shape	luster

   The paper clips can be sorted by _____ . The building

   blocks can be sorted by _____ . The colored pencils can

   be sorted by _____ .

7. Write an *M* in front of the substances that are simple mixtures. Write an *S* in front of the solutions.

_____ sugar water

_____ concrete

_____ jelly beans

_____ salt and sugar

_____ metal alloys

_____ gases

8. Which are examples of physical changes? Circle all that apply.

a. paper burning

b. paper being torn

c. wood being chopped down

d. wood burning

e. cake being cut

f. cake baking

9. Choose the correct answer. What type of change is happening in the picture to the right?

a. metal rusting; a chemical change

b. metal rusting; a physical change

c. metal rotting; a chemical change

d. metal rotting; a physical change

10. When a chemical change occurs, what do you know about the amount of matter in the new substances? What is this known as?

_____

_____

_____

_____

Energy and Matter in Organisms

Explore Online ▶

Unit Project: The Best Light
How do different kinds of light affect plant growth? You will conduct an investigation with your team to see how different kinds of light affect plants. Ask your teacher for details.

Most animals must consume other organisms to get the matter and energy they need.

At a Glance

Vocabulary Game: Picture It

Materials
• 1 set of word cards
• Timer
• Sketch pad

Directions
1. Mix up the cards face down on a table. Take turns to play.
2. Choose a card and note the word on it. Do not tell the word to the other players. Set the timer for 1 minute.
3. Draw pictures on the sketch pad to give clues about the word. Draw only pictures and numbers, use no words.
4. The first player to guess the word gets 1 point and an additional 1 point to use the word in a sentence correctly.
5. Then that player gets a turn to choose a word.
6. The first player to score 5 points wins.

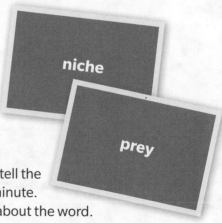

niche

prey

Unit Vocabulary

community: A group of organisms that live in the same area and interact with one another.

consumer: A living thing that cannot make its own food and must eat other living things.

ecosystem: A community of organisms and the environment in which they live.

environment: All of the living and nonliving things that surround and affect an organism.

habitat: The place where an organism lives and can find everything it needs to survive.

niche: The role that a plant or animal plays in its habitat.

photosynthesis: The process that plants use to make sugar.

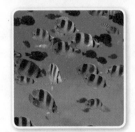

population: All the organisms of the same kind that live together in a given area.

predator: An animal that hunts, catches, and eats other animals.

prey: Animals that are caught and eaten by predators.

producer: A living thing, such as a plant, that can make its own food.

How Does Energy Get Transformed by Plants?

You may not think that plants can grow in a cave. But this forest is in a cave in Vietnam! As long as plants have what they need to grow, they can thrive in even the most unexpected places.

By the end of this lesson . . .
you'll be able to explain that plants get the materials they need to grow mostly from air and water.

Can You Explain It?

When you think about plants growing in a garden, what do you expect to see? Look at the plants in this photo. They are growing out of tubes. Think about how and where they are growing. Is this different from what you would expect?

1. You know that you need at least food and water to grow and stay healthy. What do you think plants need to grow? How are the plants in the picture able to grow without soil?

_____

_____

_____

_____

_____

_____

_____

Tip

Learn more about how matter changes in How Does Matter Change?

 EVIDENCE NOTEBOOK Look for this icon to help you gather evidence to answer the questions above.

Plant Growth

Can It Grow?

Under each caption, finish the sentence by writing what the plant is getting to meet its needs, or what it is lacking to meet its needs.

2. These plants are being

_____

_____

_____

3. This plant is in a vacuum-sealed container that does not contain any

_____

_____

_____

4. Some plants, such as this Venus Flytrap, grow in soil that does not have a lot of nutrients. The Venus Flytrap gets nutrients from consuming

_____

_____

5. Think about plants that are not getting what they need to grow. What do you think will happen to these plants?

_____

_____

_____

What Do Plants Need to Grow?

6. Think about what you've learned about what plants need to grow. Work with your group to plan an experiment. Your group might plan to test how a plant grows with no water, some water, or a lot of water. Or you might plan an experiment to compare how a plant grows with and without air. Your plan should identify the variable being tested. Include a procedure that includes a control group and an experimental group. Give directions on how to collect data, and list the materials needed.

Record your plan. Be sure to include the variable being tested, the procedure (including the control and experimental groups), the materials needed, and how data would be collected. Predict the results.

_____

_____

_____

_____

_____

_____

_____

_____

_____

_____

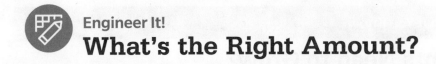

Engineer It!
What's the Right Amount?

Imagine that you were trying to grow roses in an area where it doesn't rain very often. How would you make sure the plants got enough water between rainstorms? You would probably water them with a sprinkler system or hand water them with water collected in rain barrels.

Some areas do not have a lot of water. In these areas, machines may be used to irrigate plants in the most efficient way possible so that no water is wasted.

Some areas have a lot of water. If these places are hilly or mountainous, fields may be designed to look like steps to reduce soil loss. This also allows plants that need a lot of water, like rice, to grow.

Irrigation engineers design structures to water, or irrigate, plants. One way to do this is to water plant roots. This type of system is made by burying plastic pipes with holes in them along rows of plants. These systems can be run on a timer so that irrigation occurs during cooler parts of the day. This reduces water loss due to evaporation.

7. In the space below, draw a model of an irrigation system that optimizes water use in a dry area or in a wet area.

What's Needed?

Think about two kinds of plants you've seen, such as a maple tree and a dandelion. How are these plants similar? Both have leaves and a stem and produce flowers. But how do a maple tree and a dandelion differ? The stem of a maple tree is the trunk, while a dandelion has a soft stem. Plants have similar structures that also have differences.

Saguaro cactuses live in the Sonoran Desert in the Southwest United States. Their roots are shallow, and they spread out over a large area. This helps them absorb as much water as possible when it rains. The roots only grow about 12 cm deep. They spread out to a length that is equal to the height of the plant.

The roots of this pecan tree are much larger. They grow deep into the ground and spread out over a large area compared to the diameter of the trunk. They can absorb water from deep in the ground, even when it hasn't rained for a long time. The roots of a mature pecan tree can take in between 570 and 950 L of water a day!

 8. Language SmArts Research more about how too much water can affect plant growth. Use more than one print or digital source to find information. Write your findings below.

_____

_____

_____

_____

Do the Math
Thirsty Trees

9. A saguaro cactus can absorb 760 L of water during a heavy storm. A pecan tree can absorb 570,000 mL per day. Convert the units to determine which plant absorbs the larger amount of water.

_____

_____

Next, circle the plant that correctly completes the sentence.

The saguaro cactus/pecan tree takes in the most water at a time.

The saguaro lives in places that are very dry but have rare, heavy rainstorms that may occur once a month. It absorbs 760 L of water during one such storm. The pecan tree takes in the 570,000 mL it needs each day during its growing season. Which plant requires more water over time? Explain your reasoning.

_____

_____

_____

 EVIDENCE NOTEBOOK In your Evidence Notebook, identify whether plants that do not need a lot of water or plants that do need a lot of water would grow better in your area. Explain your answer. Suppose the type of plant best suited to your area is a plant that does not need a lot of water. What could you do to grow such a plant in your area?

Putting It Together

10. These plants are growing on the International Space Station! How are the plants getting what they need to grow? What do you think would happen if the plants were released into space?

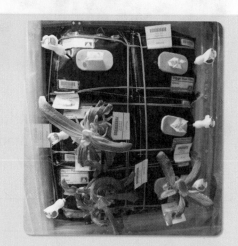

_____

_____

_____

_____

Lights Out!

You have learned that plants need water and air to survive. Plants also need nutrients. What else do plants need to survive and grow?

Objective

Collaborate to collect data about how light is related to plant growth and survival.

What question will you investigate to meet this objective?

_____

_____

Materials

- 2 small potted plants
- masking tape
- marker
- measuring cup
- water
- metric ruler
- graph paper
- colored pencils

Procedure

STEP 1 Use the tape and marker to label one plant "Regular Light" and one plant "No Light."

Why is it important to label the plants?

_____

_____

_____

_____

STEP 2 Place one plant in front of a window getting regular light. Place the other plant in a cabinet 24 hours a day for the length of the experiment.

Why did you put the plants in different places?

_____

_____

STEP 3 Water both plants every three days. Use the same amount of water for each plant.

Why is it important to give all the plants the same amount of water?

_____

_____

_____

STEP 4 Use the metric ruler to measure the height of each plant every other day. Make observations about the appearance of the plants' stem and leaves as well.

Complete the data table as you carry out the experiment.

Day	Regular Light		No Light	
	Height (cm)	Observations	Height (cm)	Observations
1				
3				
5				
7				
9				
11				

STEP 5 At the end of the experiment, clean up as instructed by your teacher.

Why is it important to dispose of or recycle the plants properly?

_____

_____

_____

_____

_____

Analyze Your Results

STEP 6 Make a graph of your results on graph paper. Label the x-axis "Time (Days)" and the "y-axis Growth (cm)." Use two different color pencils to graph the results for each plant on the graph. Be sure to include a key and a title for your graph. Then submit your completed graph to your teacher.

STEP 7 What variable did you test in this experiment? Which plant was the control plant?

_____

_____

STEP 8 Collaborate with other teams. Compare your results to those of your classmates. Were your results similar to those of other groups? Why or why not?

_____

_____

STEP 9 What differences in growth did you observe?

_____

_____

STEP 10 What other differences did you observe among the plants?

_____

_____

Draw Conclusions

STEP 11 Make a claim about the effect of light on plants. Cite evidence to support your claim.

_____

_____

STEP 12 What is one question you still have about how light affects plant growth?

_____

_____

Getting Energy from Food

Who Needs Food?

So far, you've learned that plants need water, air, and light to grow and survive. But how do they use the water, air, and light? Well, plants need food, but they don't eat other plants to get food. So how do plants get the food they need?

Making Food

11. The lettered captions show each step in this process. Study the picture and the captions, then match each caption to the step it describes in the picture.

Explore Online

a. Plants absorb water through their roots. The water then moves up into the stem and leaves of a plant.

b. Plant have structures that capture light energy from the sun.

c. Plants get carbon dioxide from the air.

d. Using light energy, plants then change carbon dioxide and water into sugar and oxygen.

Plants change carbon dioxide and water into oxygen and sugar through a process called photosynthesis. Light energy from the sun is needed for photosynthesis to take place.

Plants make the food they need to survive and grow by carrying out photosynthesis. This food contains energy stored as matter. The matter in the food is made up of sugars and comes from the carbon dioxide in the air and water. The energy stored in the sugars was once light energy from the sun. Oxygen is released as a waste material into the air.

In and Out

Plants need to take in carbon dioxide from air. They also need to release oxygen into the air. How do they do this? To find out, look at this picture of a plant leaf under a microscope. The underside of a leaf has openings called *stomata*. Carbon dioxide and oxygen move into and out of a plant through stomata when they are open.

There are structures on the sides of the stomata. The structures control whether the stomata are open or not. When these structures are swollen, the stomata are open. When they are shriveled, the stomata are closed.

12. You have learned that a plant needs carbon dioxide, water, and light to carry out photosynthesis. You've explored the plant parts that take in each of these. Now, apply what you've learned to make a model that shows all of the parts of a plant that are involved in photosynthesis. Don't forget to include parts that are too small to see without a microscope. Sketch your model in the space below.

Picture This!

13. Study the diagram below. It shows the things a plant needs to carry out photosynthesis, as well as the things produced by photosynthesis. Write the terms in the correct places on the diagram.

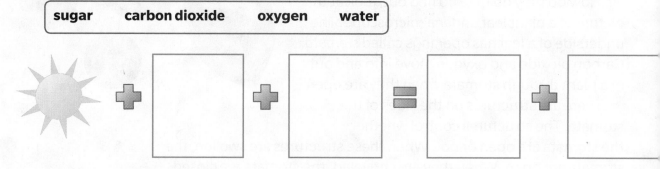

sugar   carbon dioxide   oxygen   water

14. Which two things do all plants need for photosynthesis? Choose the correct answer.

a. carbon dioxide and soil

c. insects and water

b. water and carbon dioxide

d. soil and sugar

 EVIDENCE NOTEBOOK Look at the illustration of the stomata again. In your Evidence Notebook, explain how stomata help a plant get the materials it needs to grow. Describe what would happen if a plant did not have stomata.

 Language SmArts
Use Visual Displays

15. You've learned that plants need air, water, and energy from the sun to make food to grow and survive. Explain how plants get each of these. Then explain how plants use these to make food.

_____

_____

_____

_____

_____

_____

_____

> **Tip**
>
> The English Language Arts Handbook can provide help with understanding how to use visual displays to demonstrate information about main ideas.

Discover More

Check out this path . . . or go online to choose one of these other paths.

People in Science & Engineering

- **Not Only Plants!**
- **Design Your Own Hydroponics System**

A Moss-Powered Radio

Fabienne Felder is a designer. Dr. Paolo Bombelli, Dr. Chris Howe, and Ross Dennis are scientists. These four people have worked together to make fuel cells—using plants to generate electricity!

Dr. Chris Howe is a biochemist at the University of Cambridge. His science lab is leading the way on research for moss-powered radios.

Fabienne Felder is a designer from Switzerland. She originated the concept and design of the radio using Howe's technology.

Dr. Paolo Bombelli, a biochemist at the University of Cambridge, is the leading researcher on the science team.

Ross Dennis, a plant scientist at the University of Cambridge, is a key collaborator on the project.

By using the electrical power generated when plants carry out photosynthesis, they can make a radio work in the same way as if it were plugged into a socket in the wall. The team hopes to be able to design systems that generate enough power to charge cell phones or provide electricity to the part of an airplane where the passengers sit.

After working with moss, the team discovered some of its limitations. For example, it cannot get too much light and it does not grow well in cold temperatures. This has led them to more questions, such as the following:

Moss-powered radio

- Which are the best types of plants to use?

- How much light do the plants need?

- What are the best conditions in which the plants grow?

- What are the best types of materials that can be used to conduct electricity?

- How can the plants be cared for and kept healthy while still having the overall system provide a steady stream of electricity?

16. Think about the issues the scientists encountered. Their vision for the future is to have plants cover large surfaces, and the system will provide electricity. How do you think some of these issues can be solved? Is the type or size of the plant important? Why or why not?

_____

_____

_____

_____

_____

17. Why is it important to consider the care and health of the plants? Why is it important that the electricity is produced in the most efficient way possible? How could the team answer some of these questions?

_____

_____

_____

_____

Lesson Check

Name _____

Can You Explain It?

1. Now that you've learned more about what plants need to grow and survive, explain how the plants in the image are so healthy. Be sure to do the following:

   • Describe what plants need to survive.

   • Explain how plants make their own food.

   • Explain how these plants are growing even though they aren't being grown in soil.

EVIDENCE NOTEBOOK Use the information you've collected in your Evidence Notebook to help you answer these questions.

_____

_____

_____

_____

_____

_____

_____

_____

Checkpoints

2. Draw a line matching each term to whether it is needed for photosynthesis or produced by photosynthesis.

carbon dioxide

oxygen

Needed for photosynthesis		Produced by photosynthesis

sugar

sunlight

water

Use the illustration below to answer the questions.

3. Suppose the two plants in the photograph are getting the same amount of sunlight, air, and nutrients. What could cause the first plant to look the way it does? Choose all that apply.

   a. It is getting too much sun.

   b. It is not getting enough air.

   c. It is getting too much water.

   d. It is not getting enough water.

4. Suppose one of the plants is only getting 2 hours of sunlight every 24 hours. Which plant is that? Assume that all other conditions are the same for each plant. Choose the best answer.

   a. The first plant, because it is not getting enough light to make enough food

   b. The first plant,, because it is not getting enough air to make enough food

   c. The second plant, because it is not getting enough light to make enough food

   d. The second plant, because it is not getting enough air to make enough food.

5. What is true of maple trees and saguaro cactuses? Choose all that apply.

   a. They are the same size.

   b. They grow in different climates.

   c. They have different root systems.

   d. They need the same amount of water.

6. Match each sentence to the step it describes on the illustration shown here.

   a. Light energy from the sun is captured by structures in leaves.

   b. Roots absorb water from soil.

   c. Stomata allow the plant to take in carbon dioxide and release oxygen.

Lesson Roundup

A. Choose the words that correctly complete the sentences.

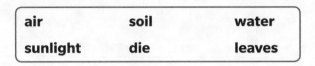

air	soil	water
sunlight	die	leaves

Plants need _____ , which they take in through stomata.

Plants also need _____ , which they absorb through their roots. If

plants do not get enough water, their _____ will wilt. If plants do

not get any air, they will _____ .

B. Study the diagram below. It shows the things needed for photosynthesis and the things produced by photosynthesis in the wrong order. Redraw the diagram, placing the items in correct order.

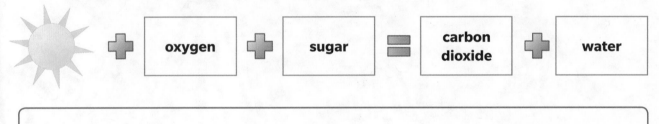

C. Write anything else you learned about how plants use energy from the sun to change matter that isn't food into matter that is food!

_____

_____

_____

_____

How Do Organisms Use Matter and Energy?

This monarch butterfly changes throughout its lifetime. What does it need from its environment to change and develop?

By the end of this lesson . . .
you'll be able to explain how organisms use matter and energy obtained from their environments.

Can You Explain It?

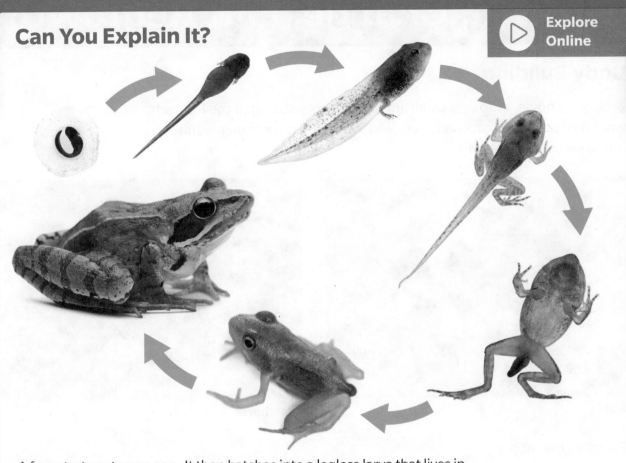

A frog starts out as an egg. It then hatches into a legless larva that lives in water. It swims with a tail and breathes with gills. As it grows, legs develop. The tail is absorbed by its body, and it gradually loses its gills. Eventually, the frog is able to live and breathe on land.

1. What is this frog made of? How do you think it gets the raw materials that make its body and fuel its activities?

_____

_____

_____

_____

_____

_____

Tip

Learn more about how energy from the sun is captured in How Does Energy Get Transformed by Plants?

 EVIDENCE NOTEBOOK Look for this icon to help you gather evidence to answer the questions above.

Growth, Change, and Regrowth

Body Building

A baby horse, or foal, is small and not yet very strong. If the foal gets what it needs, it will grow and develop into a large, muscular, adult horse with a strong body.

foal

adult horse

Select all that apply.

2. What do you think a foal needs to grow into an adult horse?

   a. air

   b. water

   c. a barn

   d. nutrients

   e. hay for bedding

   f. food

   g. grooming

   h. a saddle

Growth and repair of body parts requires matter, which for animals are raw materials. When food is eaten, matter is broken down into simpler forms. These can be used to build or repair an animal's body.

Growth, repair, and other life processes also require energy. When food matter is broken down, energy is released. The animal's body can then use the energy.

 3. Language SmArts Animals require matter, such as oxygen, food, and water, to survive. Why do they need matter? What do you think might happen if an animal cannot access one of them?

_____

_____

_____

Taking It All In

4. Although animals come in different shapes and sizes, they all need matter and energy for growth and repair. Look at the images of different animals getting what they need from their environments. Use the words in the word bank to complete the descriptions.

Explore Online

air	water	food

All animals need to exchange gases with their surroundings. Different animals have different structures for gas exchange. A mammal, such as this polar bear, has lungs for taking in oxygen from the

_____ and breathing out carbon dioxide as waste. An animal's circulatory system carries oxygen throughout its body.

Birds, like all animals, have ways of getting _____ from the environment. Without water, animals cannot survive. In fact, most animal bodies have a great deal of water in them. Once used, the water an organism consumes is released back into the environment as waste.

As this lizard feeds on the plant, its body breaks down the plant matter. The matter is digested into raw materials that are used to build structures and repair damaged body parts. The breakdown of _____ also releases energy that can be used for life processes, such as motion to find more things to eat.

Producers to Consumers

Animals drink and eat food to obtain the matter and energy they need for their life processes. Some organisms, such as plants, can make their own food. An organism that makes its own food is called a **producer.** Plants are able to use the energy from sunlight to produce sugars, which are a source of energy and matter.

On the other hand, an animal cannot make its own food. An animal is a **consumer,** an organism that obtains energy and matter by feeding on other organisms. Animals are consumers and get what they need from the environment.

A bird may obtain matter and energy by eating fruits, seeds, insects, or other small animals. It drinks water it can find and obtains oxygen from the environment, too. Wastes are released back into the environment.

5. Which of the following do you think an animal can live without?

   a. air   **c.** water

   b. food   **d.** none of the above

While animals take in matter from the environment, they also release wastes into the environment. Wastes are produced when matter is converted into materials that are not used by the body. Some wastes are from the breakdown of food. Others may be by-products from life processes. Wastes are then released into the environment.

For example, carbon dioxide gas is a waste product released when an animal breathes out. Animals also eliminate the remains of digested food out of the body as waste.

6. What happens to materials that are taken in but not used by the body?

   a. They are changed into materials that are needed.

   b. They are stored forever in the body.

   c. They are released into the environment as waste.

Snails use the matter they obtain from food in many ways. Unused matter is released from the body.

 EVIDENCE NOTEBOOK In your Evidence Notebook, make a list of some ways animals get their food. What are some sources of food for an animal?

Do the Math

Growing Anew

Some animals can regenerate, or regrow, body parts. Regenerating body parts requires energy and matter. Food is important to an animal not only for growth but also for body repair.

Although only a few animals have the ability to regrow limbs, all animals perform body repair. Body repair can be as simple as producing substances to help a cut heal or as complex as repairing a broken bone.

Explore Online

When a sea star's arm is damaged or lost, it can grow a new one! In some cases, a sea star can even regrow its entire body.

7. Using the graph, find the average rate of regrowth of a sea star's arm. Is this average rate a good indicator of its arm length after 4 months?

_____

_____

_____

_____

_____

_____

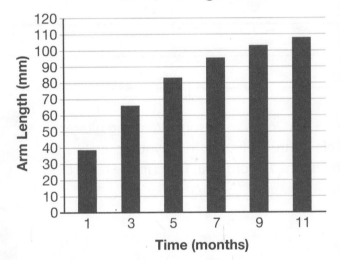

Sea Star Arm Regeneration

Putting It Together

You've learned that animals need food to supply materials for body growth and repair. You've also learned that animals obtain gases and water from the environment and release waste matter back into the environment.

8. Name two reasons why animals need food to live, and explain your answers.

_____

_____

HANDS-ON ACTIVITY

What Was for Dinner?

Objective

No matter what an animal eats, the animal is consuming its food to obtain energy that is then stored as matter. This energy is needed because it is used for body repair, growth, motion, and maintaining body warmth. Think about different foods you can eat that provide the most energy.

Collaborate with your group to determine what fruit has the most energy.

What question will you investigate to meet this objective?

_____

_____

_____

Materials
- selection of fruits and vegetables
- balance
- nutrition information
- gloves
- paper plates
- calculator

STEP 1 Work in a group. Wearing gloves, select three different fruits you would like to compare. Record your fruits in the table below.

Fruit	Weight (gram)	Calories per 10 grams	Total calories per fruit

STEP 2 Peel any fruits where the peels are not typically eaten.

Why are you peeling some of the fruits but not others before using them?

_____

_____

_____

STEP 3 Use the balance to determine the weight of the fruit in grams. Make sure to consider the weight of the plate when determining the weight of the fruit. Measure the fruit at least twice for accuracy and record the weights in the table.

A calorie is the unit used to measure food energy. Which fruit do you think has the highest calorie per gram?

_____

_____

_____

STEP 4 Once you've completed Step 3, get the nutrition information from your teacher. Use the nutrition information provided to determine how many calories per gram each of your fruits has.

Which piece of fruit has the most calories in it?

_____

_____

_____

_____

Analyze Your Results

STEP 5   Which kind of fruit provides the most energy?

_____

_____

_____

_____

STEP 6   Collaborate with other groups that selected different fruits to determine which fruits had the most energy. Write the types of fruit and their calories below.

_____

_____

_____

_____

STEP 7   Using the information from Steps 5 and 6, draw a bar graph showing each piece of fruit and the amount of energy per gram that it stores.

STEP 8 What is one thing you notice about fruits that are high energy?

_____

_____

_____

Draw Conclusions

STEP 9 While some fruits may have more energy in them, animals may choose to eat other fruits that have less energy. Why do you think they do this?

_____

_____

_____

STEP 10 Make a claim about which fruits are the highest.

_____

_____

STEP 11 Cite evidence to support your claim.

_____

_____

_____

STEP 12 What other questions do you have about how animals use energy from food?

_____

_____

_____

Animal Energy

Brrr! It's cold outside!

Animals need food so they have the matter and energy they need for their bodies to grow, develop, and repair themselves. Food helps animals survive in other ways as well. How might food help an animal survive in an extreme environment such as the Antarctic?

Explore Online

It's bitterly cold in the Antarctic, where many penguins make their home. Here, temperatures may be "high" at –20 °C in the summer and dip below –60 °C in the winter! So how do these penguins stay warm? By eating! In addition to providing matter and energy for growth and body repair, food provides energy to keep their bodies warm.

Do the Math
Counting Krill Calories

An adult Adélie penguin eats about 0.9 kg of krill each summer day. An individual krill weighs about 2 grams. Each gram of krill has 0.9 calories available for whichever predator eats it. A calorie is the amount of energy available from food.

9. Using the data provided, calculate how many calories an Adélie penguin eats in a typical summer day.

_____

_____

_____

Energy on the Move

10. The sun shines down on a sunflower. Read the captions below the image, and then label the art with the appropriate caption letters.

Explore Online

a. An *aphid* is an insect that feeds on plant sap with its piercing, sucking mouthparts. They tap directly into the system of tubes that carries water and sugars throughout the plant. Aphids use these sugars as food to fuel their own body functions.

b. Whoosh! A *wasp* flies down, catches an aphid, and then munches on it as food. From the aphid, the wasp will obtain matter and energy to fuel its own life processes, including growth and flight.

c. *Sunflower* leaves capture the energy from sunlight to power the process of photosynthesis. Energy from sunlight is used by the plant to change carbon dioxide and water into sugars. The plant uses the energy stored in the sugars as fuel for its life processes.

d. The *sun* provides the energy that producers, such as plants, need to make their own food. This energy is provided in the form of sunlight, which travels from the sun to Earth as solar energy.

11. Where did the wasp's energy *originally* come from?

a. aphid

b. water

c. plant sap

d. sunlight

The original source of energy for nearly all organisms on Earth comes from the sun. Some organisms, such as those in dark environments, are able to use energy from sources other than the sun.

Where's the Heat?

Check the room temperature using a thermometer. Write down your observations. Now use the provided forehead thermometer strips to check your own body temperature. Record your readings. Collaborate with classmates to compare your results.

12. What can you conclude about body temperature compared to room temperature? Where do you think the energy that is keeping your body warm comes from?

_____

_____

_____

 EVIDENCE NOTEBOOK Think about how energy and matter are important for animals. In what ways are energy and matter connected? In your Evidence Notebook, list the sources of energy and the sources of matter for animals.

 Language SmArts
Use the Internet

Tip

The English Language Arts Handbook can provide help with understanding how to use the Internet.

13. You have learned that energy from the sun gets transferred to producers first and then up the food chain through consumers. It might be surprising to think that this applies even to the largest animal on Earth. Use digital resources to research what the largest animal on Earth today is and what it eats. Then, in your own words, describe how the animal relies, ultimately, on the energy of the sun.

_____

_____

_____

_____

Discover More

Check out this path . . . or go online to choose one of these other paths.

Careers in Science

- **In the Water**
- **Engineer It: Feed Me Now!**

Animal Nutritionist

Explore Online

Animal nutritionists study the food requirements and effects of different nutrients on animals. They may help develop the diet for animals, making sure the animals get what they need. Animal nutritionists work at a variety of places, including universities, pet food companies, zoos, farms, and animal rehabilitation centers.

This nutritionist is bottle feeding a baby squirrel to make sure it gets the nourishment it needs to grow healthy and strong.

Choose an animal you are interested in. Make a list of its characteristics that you are interested in learning more about. Then do research to learn about these characteristics, as well as what and how much the animal eats in the wild.

14. Which animal did you choose? What are some of its characteristics?

_____

_____

_____

15. Where does your chosen animal live? What does it eat?

_____

_____

_____

16. Design a menu such as the ones you see at restaurants for your animal meal plan.

Lesson Check

Name _____

Can You Explain It?

Explore Online

1. See how dramatically the frog's body changes! What do frogs—and all animals— need in order for their bodies to grow, develop, and repair themselves? How do they use these materials for bodily processes? Be sure to do the following:

   • Describe the roles of energy and matter in body processes.

   • Explain why animals need food.

   • Identify the source of the energy in food.

EVIDENCE NOTEBOOK Use the information you've collected in your Evidence Notebook to help answer these questions.

_____

_____

_____

_____

_____

_____

_____

Checkpoints

2. Study the photo to answer the question. What is the original source of energy used to make the food this horse is eating?

   a. air

   b. water

   c. grass

   d. sun

3. Use the words below to fill in the table of producers and consumers.

tree	dog	lettuce	whale
grass	lizard	octopus	chicken

Producer	Consumer

4. Use the words in the word bank to complete three different diagrams depicting the movement of energy. One word will be used more than once.

sunlight	aphid	sunflower
rabbit	hawk	chicken
corn	wasp	clover

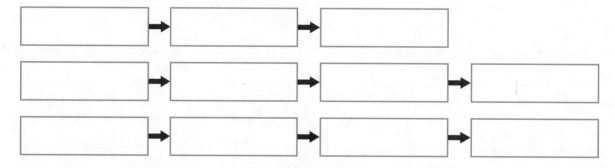

5. For which of the following do animals use the energy in food?

a. growth

c. motion

b. repair

d. photosynthesis

6. Which of the following meals would offer the most energy to a consumer?

a. 2 bananas at 105 calories each, plus one avocado at 322 calories

b. half a coconut at 1,406 calories per whole coconut

c. half a watermelon at 1,372 calories per whole melon, plus one cup of cranberries at 46 calories per cup

d. two steaks at 345 calories each

Lesson Roundup

A. Choose the correct answer for each sentence.

consumers	**eating other organisms**	**producers**
waste matter	**drinking water**	**oxygen**

Animals are _____ that get the materials necessary for

body growth and repair by _____. Animals obtain gases and

water from the environment and release _____ back into the

environment.

B. Choose the correct answer for each sentence.

consumers	**sugars**	**sun**
producers	**water**	**carbon dioxide**

Plants are _____ that can use the sun's energy to make

_____, which they use as food. When an animal eats plants

or eats another animal that eats plants, it is getting energy that originally came

from the _____.

How Do Organisms Interact?

In the winter months, resources such as food and shelter may be limited in certain ecosystems. While bears and wolves don't typically consume one another, often times they interact when competing for food.

By the end of this lesson . . .
you'll understand how organisms interact.

Can You Explain It?

Explore
Online

Look at these animals near this dried-out watering hole. How are they interacting with each other and their environment? Will these animals be able to survive if they cannot meet their need for water?

1. What do you think will happen to the animals in the photo above? How do you think they can find the resources they need?

_____

_____

_____

_____

_____

_____

_____

_____

_____

Tip

Learn more about what organisms need to survive in How Do Organisms Use Energy?

 EVIDENCE NOTEBOOK Look for this icon to help you gather evidence to answer the questions above.

197

Living Things and Their Environment

It's Alive!

There are both living things and nonliving things in nearly every environment. Living things, such as plants an animals, interact with other living things for food and shelter. Living things also depend on the nonliving parts of the environment. Living things, also called *organisms,* include plants, animals, and bacteria. Nonliving things include rocks, water, and air.

Living Together

2. Study the picture. Circle the living things in this ecosystem.

The living things in the image live in a forest environment. An **environment** is made up of all the living and nonliving things that surround and affect an organism. The black bear is affected by the other living things in the picture. The bear is also affected by nonliving things, such as climate, water, soil, light, air, and nutrients. This forest is an ecosystem. An **ecosystem** is a community of organisms and the environment in which they live.

HANDS-ON Apply What You Know

What's in Your Environment?

3. Develop three interview questions that you could use to find out more about your classmates' environments. Be sure to ask about both living and nonliving parts of the environment. Use your questions to interview several classmates. Then, summarize what you have learned about your classmates' environments. How are the environments similar? How are they different? Submit your findings to your teacher.

Engineer It!
Let's Clean Up!

Have you ever noticed trash or other wastes outside? Animals can be affected when human pollution or wastes change an environment. Pollution can affect water, air, and land. Select one specific place or environment that is affected by pollution. Research the place to learn more about the impact of pollution on the living things and nonliving things there. Find out about the kinds of pollution that are found in this place.

Then, brainstorm ideas for a device that could be used to clean up pollution in the place you researched. Design a model of the device. When you are finished, turn your model in to your teacher.

4. Do you think your device would do a good job of cleaning up pollution in the real world? Why or why not?

_____

_____

_____

_____

EVIDENCE NOTEBOOK You've learned about the ways that living things interact with one another and with other parts of their environment. In your Evidence Notebook, identify factors that all species need in a healthy ecosystem. Be sure to consider plants as well as animals as you think about characteristics of a healthy ecosystem.

Wide or Narrow?

How would you describe an animal? You might talk about how it looks or moves. Another way to describe an animal is to tell where it lives, what it eats, and other ways it interacts with its environment. A **habitat** is the place where an organism lives and can find everything it needs to survive. Organisms also have a **niche** (NICH), which is the role a plant or an animal plays in its habitat.

Some organisms have a wide niche. They can live in a variety of places, eat many foods, and be a part of many different ecosystems. Other organisms have a narrow niche. They can live only in very specific places and eat one or two kinds of food.

Which Niche Is Which?

5. Study the pictures, and read the captions. Afterwards, write a *W* on the pictures of organisms with wide niches. Write an *N* on the pictures of organisms with narrow niches.

Tiger salamanders are found in many places in North America. They eat many different foods, such as frogs, worms, insects, and small mammals.

Raccoons live in a great variety of habitats, including prairies, forests, marshes, and large cities. They eat all kinds of food, ranging from frogs to fruit. Raccoons will even eat garbage!

Many kinds of cockroaches are found in different places around the world. They live in forests or even in people's homes. They will eat anything, including wallpaper paste!

Eucalyptus trees produce sugars and oxygen through photosynthesis. They grow in limited areas, and because they can be toxic, provide food and a home for only a few animals.

The Difference Is Night and Day

Animals that live in the same habitat usually have different niches. This allows each animal to get what it needs from the environment. What do you think would happen if the animals had the same niche?

Red-shouldered hawks are hunters. They live in forest habitats and catch prey such as snakes, frogs, and mice to eat. Red-shouldered hawks mostly hunt and catch their prey during the day.

The barred owl also lives in forest habitats. It hunts and eats the same types of prey that the red-shouldered hawk eats. Owls hunt at night and at dawn and dusk.

6. Language SmArts You have discovered that red-shouldered hawks and barred owls share the same habitat. They hunt for the same kinds of food. Apply what you have learned about niches to explain how these organisms can both get what they need from their shared habitat.

_____

_____

_____

Putting It Together

7. The natural habitat of black bears is a forest. As humans have cleared forests for construction and homes, bears have changed their diets. How do you think the bears' niche has changed as its habitat has been changed by humans?

_____

_____

_____

_____

_____

What's Out There?

Objective

Many environments and ecosystems are very large. They include numerous species interacting in different ways. How do scientists observe all the interactions of the living things in a large area? How might they go about identifying and counting which species are in an ecosystem? Scientists sometimes survey part of an area and then use their results to estimate the populations of those species in an area.

Materials
- gloves
- string
- wooden dowels
- meterstick or other measuring device
- collecting jar
- scissors
- hand lens
- field guides for the local environment

Collaborate with your group members to study the components of an ecosystem and how they interact. Use scientific methods to estimate the populations of different species.

What question will you investigate to meet this objective?

_____

_____

Procedure

STEP 1 Work in a group. With your group, measure and cut a 4.5-meter length of string.

How will you use your length of string to study a part of an ecosystem?

_____

_____

_____

You'll be making a square with a 4-meter perimeter. What is the length of each side of the square? Why did you need to cut a length of string 4.5 m long?

_____

_____

STEP 2 Take your equipment, including the measured string, to a place specified by your teacher. Wearing gloves, use the meterstick to measure out a square meter. Put a wooden post in the ground at each corner of the square. Wrap the string around each post to make the sides of square on the ground. Tie a knot at the end.

Each group in your class will study a different square, but all the squares will be the same size. Why is it important that they are all the same size?

_____

_____

_____

STEP 3 Observe and record the number and types of living things in your group's square. Use the hand lens and collecting jar to observe very small organisms. Use the field guide or the Internet to help identify unknown plants and animals.

What are some living things you observe in your square?

_____

_____

_____

Total number of organisms observed	
Number of producers observed	
Number of consumers observed	

Analyze Your Results

STEP 4 Did your group observe more producers or more consumers?

_____

_____

_____

STEP 5 Compare your results to the results of other groups. Describe any similarities or differences you notice.

_____

_____

_____

STEP 6 In this activity, you observed and counted the living things in a one-square-meter part of the ecosystem. How do you think your results would be similar or different if you tried to count every living thing in the whole ecosystem? Why wouldn't you count all the living things? Cite evidence.

_____

_____

_____

Draw Conclusions

STEP 7 Make a claim about why scientists study ecosystems in sections.

_____

_____

Cite evidence to support your claim.

_____

_____

STEP 8 What other questions do you have about the ways in which scientists study ecosystems?

_____

_____

_____

Relationships in an Ecosystem

What Group Are You In?

The living things in an ecosystem interact with one another. Living things live with other organisms and nonliving things in the ecosystem.

Populations and Communities

8. Study the pictures and read the captions below. Then circle the living things and draw squares around the nonliving things in the images.

Explore Online

A group of organisms of the same kind in an ecosystem, like this herd of elephants, is called a **population**. The members of a population interact with one another. They have very similar needs. They eat the same kind of food and need the same kind of shelter. They all need water and space to grow and find food. The members of a population interact as they meet their needs.

The different populations that share an ecosystem make up a community. A **community** consists of all the populations that live and can interact in an area. The living things in a community might not have all of the same needs. Even if they have different needs, the populations in a community interact.

Calculate Energy Units

9. You have been asked to help the owners of a nature preserve decide if they have enough land to support a community of zebra and antelope. In order for the animals to get what they need, 2 acres of land are needed for each zebra, and $\frac{1}{2}$ acre of land is needed for each antelope. The preserve is 420 acres in size. The preserve owners would like to have 200 zebra and 60 antelope in the preserve.

Will the preserve have enough space to accommodate all of these animals? If not, how many more acres of land will they need? If they do have enough land, could additional zebra and antelope be added?

_____

_____

_____

_____

_____

_____

_____

10. What will happen in an ecosystem if there are not enough resources to support all of the populations of living things found there? Choose all that apply.

   a. Some living things might move to a new ecosystem.

   b. Many more living things will move into the ecosystem.

   c. Some living things might die.

   d. More resources will be produced to meet the demands of the living things.

   e. Some living things will struggle to get what they need.

Resources in any ecosystem are limited. There is only so much space available in an ecosystem. There are limited amounts of water and of food. Since space, water, and food are limited, they may be _limiting factors_. Limiting factors limit how many living things of a particular population an ecosystem can support.

Limited Supply

The living things in an ecosystem often have to compete with one another to get what they need to survive. Individuals and populations that compete successfully will get the resources they need. They will survive. Individuals and populations that do not compete successfully cannot get what they need. They will not survive unless they move.

Food is a resource that all animals need to survive. Look at the pictures to see how some animals get the food they need.

Snack Time!

11. Study the pictures, and read the captions. Underline the name of the animal that hunts, and circle the name of the animal that is hunted in each caption.

Grizzly bears eat many types of food. It isn't uncommon to find them catching and eating salmon in the rivers.

Some insects eat other animals. This dragonfly is getting food by catching and eating a wasp.

Snakes need to hunt for their food. This snake gets the food it needs by catching and eating mice.

Eat or Be Eaten

You've read that the living things in an ecosystem interact. You've seen that competition for resources is one way populations interact. The pictures on the previous page showed another kind of interaction—the interaction between predators and prey.

Predators are animals that hunt, catch, and eat other animals to get the food they need. **Prey** are the animals they catch and eat. In an ecosystem, predator and prey populations interact.

12. Which organisms are predators? Choose all that apply.

   a. a wolf that eats a moose

   b. a rabbit that eats grass

   c. a mouse that eats seeds

   d. a bird that eats worms

 EVIDENCE NOTEBOOK Research two living things that have similar niches in the same environment. In your Evidence Notebook, explain how limiting factors affect and control the sizes of the populations of these living things.

 Language SmArts
Making Inferences

13. Research and compare two populations that compete in an ecosystem. Identify the resource or resources for which the populations compete.

_____

_____

_____

_____

_____

 Tip

The English Language Arts Handbook can provide help with understanding how to conduct research and using multiple resources.

Discover More

Check out this path . . . or go online to choose one of these other paths.

People in Science & Engineering

- Engineer It! Tiny Ecosystems
- Animal Atlas

It's All Fun and Games

Dr. John Weishampel is a researcher and professor at the University of Central Florida. He studies how the nonliving and living parts of ecosystems interact. He often uses scientific models to explore interactions in different ecosystems. These models, called simulations, are based on collected data.

Dr. John Weishampel

The GAMES Lab at the University of Central Florida sounds like a place to go to play games and have fun. But, the letters in the word *GAMES* stand for the Geospatial Analysis and Modeling of Ecological Systems laboratory. It's a place where data are used to make models of ecosystems. These models help researchers better understand how the parts of an ecosystem interact.

Dr. Tanya Berger-Wolf also uses data and computers to model the interactions in ecosystems. She uses both computer science and life science in her work. The models are developed at the Laboratory for Computational Population Biology at the University of Illinois at Chicago. In this lab, models are developed for processes that are hard to observe in person, such as the movement of baboons through their habitat.

Dr. Tanya Berger-Wolf

Research an ecology simulation game that is available online. Use your teacher's guidelines for research, and have your teacher approve the game you find. Then, explore the simulation. Use it to find out more about the interactions in ecosystems. After you are familiar with how the simulation works, think about how you could share your knowledge with others.

14. Write an instruction manual others could use to carry out a simulation. Make sure to describe the purpose of the simulation and how it is used. Draw a sample of your simulation showing what the screen should look like. Collaborate with classmates, and have them use your manual to carry out a simulation.

Lesson Check

Name _____

Can You Explain It?

1. Now that you've learned more about interactions of living things, explain what you think will happen to the animals in the photo. Be sure to do the following:

Explore Online ▶

- Describe how these animals interact with the non-living parts of their environment.

- Describe how these animals interact with the living parts of their environment.

- Explain that these organisms can only survive if their needs are met.

📋 **EVIDENCE NOTEBOOK** Use the information you've collected in your Evidence Notebook to help you answer these questions.

_____

_____

_____

_____

_____

_____

_____

_____

Checkpoints

2. Which of these best describes an animal's habitat?
   a. the role it plays in a community
   b. the resources it doesn't use
   c. the animals it competes with
   d. the place it lives

3. Sort the parts of this ecosystem as non-living or living.

rocks	black bear	water
insects	air	birch tree

Nonliving	Living

4. Which of these groups or areas include only living things? Choose all that apply.

   a. population   **d.** environment

   b. ecosystem   **e.** habitat

   c. community

5. Circle the correct answer.

Which phrase best describes the way these animals are interacting?

   a. predator and prey

   b. sharing a niche

   c. competition for the same resources

6. Which of these describe why living things compete for resources? Circle all that apply.

   a. All living things need resources to survive.

   b. Living things can create all the resources they need.

   c. The resources in an ecosystem are limited.

   d. Most living things can survive without resources.

LESSON 3

Lesson Roundup

A. Draw lines to match each term to its definition.

habitat	a community of organisms and the environment in which they live
niche	the role a plant or an animal plays in its habitat
ecosystem	all the living and nonliving things that surround and affect an organism
environment	the place where an organism lives and can find everything it needs to survive

B. Choose the correct words to complete each sentence.

predators   prey   unlimited
limited   cooperate   compete

Animals that hunt and eat other animals are called _____.

The animals that are eaten are called _____. The resources in

an ecosystem are _____, so the populations in an ecosystem

_____ to get the resources they need to survive.

C. What else have you learned about competition and predator-prey relationships?

_____
_____
_____
_____
_____

213

ENGINEER IT!
Business Has Bean Bad

You are a botanist (plant scientist) working for a vegetable company. Bean sales have fallen recently because consumers feel that your company's beans are of poor quality. You suspect that the problem lies in the water solution used to irrigate the beans. You and your team are tasked with finding a water solution that will help your bean plants grow tall and strong.

Which solution is best to grow beans?

FIND A PROBLEM: What is your team trying to determine?

_____

_____

_____

Examine the checklist at the end of this activity and be sure that you follow it as you proceed.

BRAINSTORM: Brainstorm with your team to determine five things that dissolve in or mix with water. List them here. (Do not use *soil* or *dirt*.)

_____

_____

_____

_____

RESEARCH AND ELIMINATE: Determine whether any substances on your list are toxic. Use that and other suitable criteria to narrow your list to three items. Describe how you arrived at your final list.

_____

_____

_____

_____

Complete the table. Make sure to list one more criteria and two additional constraints.

Criteria	Constraint
☐ Cannot be toxic	☐ Will need a controlled environment
☐ Substance must dissolve in water	☐ _____
☐ _____	☐ _____

MAKE A PLAN: Use the questions below as a guide for planning your water solution comparison. Discuss your plan on the lines below.

1. Where will we grow our bean plants? What materials will we use?

2. How will we make this a fair test of the different solutions?

3. What are the procedures that we will follow? How will we determine the results.

These students are designing their experiment

_____

_____

_____

COMMUNICATE: When complete, present your project to your class. Use visuals, including charts, to describe your project's purpose, procedures, and results. State conclusions and interpretations that you have drawn from your data. Ask for thoughts, ideas, and observations from your audience as you present your material.

✅ Checklist

Review your project and check off each completed item.

_____ Includes a list of all the materials used and explanations as to why they were needed.

_____ Includes a description of the procedures and explanations as to why each was necessary.

_____ Includes conclusions based on your own observations.

_____ Includes a presentation with an exchange of ideas and observations between you and your class.

Unit Review

1. Some plants have adaptations that allow them to survive in different habitats. This plant consumes insects. What condition is it adapted to? Circle the correct answer.

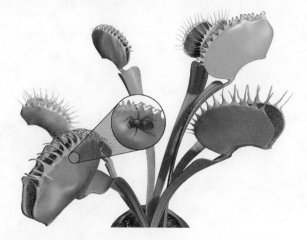

    a. a lack of water

    b. a lack of rich soil

    c. a surplus of sunshine

    d. a damaged ecosystem

2. Which of the following is a necessary part of a hydroponic system? Circle all that apply.

    a. air

    b. soil

    c. water

    d. sunlight

    e. bacteria

    f. nutrients

3. Which of the following are necessary for the process of photosynthesis in a plant to occur? Check all that apply.

    a. water

    b. sugar

    c. oxygen

    d. light energy

    e. carbon dioxide

    f. plant parts to capture the light energy

4. Food provides an organism with the matter and _____

needed for the growth and _____ of body parts.

5. Using the numbers 1–5, arrange the steps in order to describe how an organism interacts with its environment to maintain itself.

_____ Building and repairing body parts

_____ Releasing wastes into the environment

_____ Moving matter and energy throughout the body

_____ Processing matter and energy into useful forms

_____ Taking matter and energy from the environment

6. Which phrase **most** clearly describes the process occurring to the boy's arm here? Circle the correct answer.

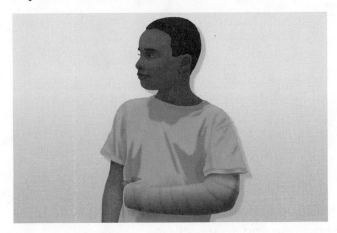

a. body repair

b. body growth

c. limb regeneration

d. energy absorption

7. Which of the following are nonliving things found in nature? Circle all that apply.

a. air

b. sand

c. moss

d. water

e. sharks

8. Indicate whether each function is performed by a plant's green structures (G), its stomata (S), or its roots (R).

Stomata

_____ Absorbing sunlight

_____ Releasing oxygen

_____ Producing sugars

_____ Absorbing water

_____ Absorbing nutrients

_____ Taking in carbon dioxide

9. Nearly all environments have animals that have either wide or narrow niches. Think of 3 animals in your neighborhood and list whether each has a wide niche or a narrow niche. Make sure to cite evidence to support your claims.

_____

_____

_____

10. Explain the difference between predators and prey. Is a predator more likely to be a producer or consumer? Explain why.

_____

_____

_____

Energy and Matter in Ecosystems

▶ Explore Online

Unit Project: Modeling an Ecosystem
How do organisms at an African watering hole interact? You will conduct an investigation with your team. Ask your teacher for details.

When organisms compete for resources, they interact in different ways.

At a Glance

Vocabulary Game: Forbidden Words

Object of The Game
• Your goal is to get your teammates to guess the vocabulary word. The team with most points wins.

Players
• groups of 4–6 players

food web
food
web
chain
many

scavenger
dead
plants
animals
food

Directions
1. You must describe your vocabulary word your teammates WITHOUT saying any of the forbidden words written on the cards. You may not use rhyming words, gestures, or drawings. You must get them to guess the correct word in less than 1 minute. If your team guesses correctly in 1 minute, you get 5 points.

2. For each forbidden word you say, deduct 1 point. It is then the next team's turn. For each forbidden word used, the team loses a point. The other team then selects a card and takes a turn.

3. Repeat until all the cards have been used. Once all the cards have been used, the team with the most points wins the game.

Unit Vocabulary

decomposer: A living thing that gets energy by breaking down dead organisms and animal wastes into simpler substances.

energy pyramid: A diagram that shows that energy is lost at each level in a food chain.

food chain: The transfer of food energy between organisms in an ecosystem.

food web: A group of food chains that overlap.

invasive species: Organism that is nonnative to an environment that disrupts the stable web of life.

scavenger: An animal that feeds on dead plants and animals.

How Do Energy and Matter Move through Ecosystems?

In a tundra ecosystem, organisms must be able to survive under extremely cold and dry conditions. Even though plant life may be scarce at times, there is still enough energy and matter to support many organisms.

By the end of this lesson . . .
you'll be able to model how energy and matter move through an ecosystem.

Can You Explain It?

 Explore Online

Local birdwatchers have been tracking an endangered owl species. The owls' food is the rabbit population, which eats grass. As the city expands, planners have taken care to not remove the trees that the owls nest in. But the birdwatchers have counted fewer owls.

1. Why do you think the owls have left the area? What do you think can be done to get them back? How would you test your idea?

_____

_____

_____

_____

_____

_____

_____

_____

_____

_____

_____

Tip

Learn more about how plants use energy from the sun in How Does Energy Get Transformed by Plants? or how animals obtain and use energy and matter in How Do Organisms Interact? and How Do Organisms Use Energy?

 EVIDENCE NOTEBOOK Look for this icon to help you gather evidence to answer the questions above.

Moving Energy and Matter

Building a Model of an Ecosystem

There are many ways in which organisms interact with each other and their environments. You've discovered that plants make their own food using energy from the sun. But how does that food matter move through an ecosystem?

Tracing Matter and Energy from Grasses to Owls

2. Using the evidence below, draw or write the names of the organisms in the circles to model how matter and energy move through the ecosystem.

 **Rabbits** are herbivores, or organisms that eat only producers, such as grass. This means they are first-level consumers.

 The **sun** is the initial source of energy for most living things on Earth.

 **Grass** uses energy from the sun to change matter that is not food into matter that is food.

 **Owls** are carnivores. This owl only eats other animals, such as rabbits. This owl is a second-level consumer

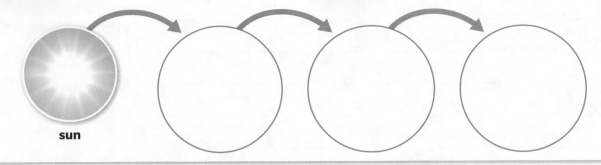

sun

All organisms in an ecosystem depend on producers to capture energy from the sun. The producers use this energy to make matter that is not food into matter that is food.

 EVIDENCE NOTEBOOK Thinking back to the beginning of the lesson, what did you notice about the amount of grass available? Using the model above, what impact do you think that has on the rabbit population? Enter your observations in your Evidence Notebook.

Explore the Tundra

A tundra ecosystem is one of the coldest and driest places on Earth. Yet many organisms thrive here. Tundra organisms rely on each other as sources of food. Explore the relationships found in the tundra ecosystem using the evidence below.

Tundra Ecosystem

Explore Online

 The **sun** supplies energy to producers so they can change matter that is not food into matter that is food.

 **Wolves** are predators. In the winter, they grow a second layer of fur for extra warmth. Animals such as caribou are their prey.

 **Caribou** eat reindeer moss and other producers to get the energy and matter they need.

 Scavengers such as this **Arctic gull** feed on the dead bodies of other plants and animals.

 **Reindeer moss** uses energy from the sun to make matter in the form of sugars from air and water.

 **Fungi and bacteria** do the cleanup work as they decompose the remains of tundra organisms.

Modeling Matter and Energy Movement

So how do energy and food matter move through a tundra ecosystem? This transfer of energy and matter from one organism to the next in an ecosystem is called a **food chain**. Each time something eats something else, food energy and matter are transferred from one organism to the next organism.

Tundra Food Chain

3. In the circles, draw or write the names of the organisms from the tundra ecosystem in the order you think energy and matter move through the food chain. You can use the evidence provided on the previous page.

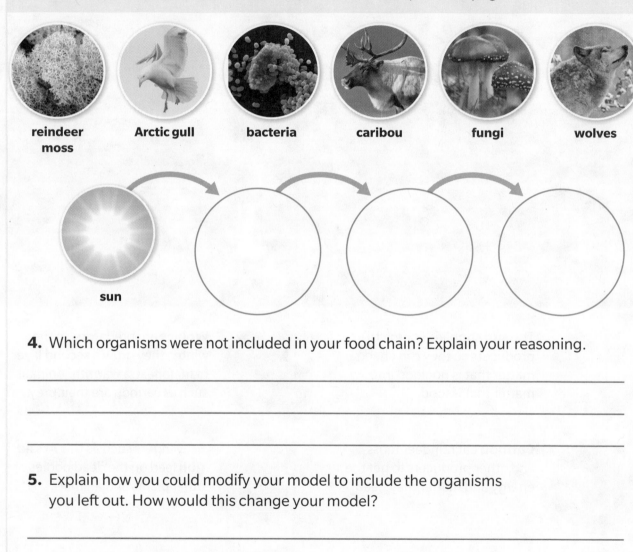

reindeer moss   Arctic gull   bacteria   caribou   fungi   wolves

sun

4. Which organisms were not included in your food chain? Explain your reasoning.

_____

_____

_____

5. Explain how you could modify your model to include the organisms you left out. How would this change your model?

_____

_____

_____

_____

Scavengers and Decomposers Are Important

Have you ever wondered about what happens to the bodies of plants and animals after they die? When plants and animals die, some organisms in the environment consume them for matter and energy.

Arctic raven

Scavengers

Arctic ravens are **scavengers**. Scavengers are consumers that eat dead organisms. Some scavengers mainly feed on the remains of dead animals. Others mainly feed on dead plants.

bacteria close-up

Decomposers

Bacteria are tiny **decomposers**. Decomposers use chemicals called enzymes to break down the remains of organisms and animal wastes. They use the energy they obtain to carry out life processes and restore materials back into the soil.

club fungi

Fungi are also decomposers that release enzymes. These enzymes break down dead matter, releasing nutrients that enrich the soil. Club fungi are one example of this kind of decomposer.

6. Which of the following organisms break the wastes down even further after scavengers are done with them? Circle the pictures of all that apply.

a. fungi

b. bacteria

c. wolves

d. lemmings

Language SmArts
Making Inferences

7. How does the leftover matter and energy in dead organisms get recycled back to the soil? Which organism in the tundra food chain would use this recycled matter? Use evidence from the tundra food chain to support your inference.

_____

_____

_____

_____

Following Matter and Energy

Connecting Food Chains

In the last section, you saw that a food chain can show how an animal gets its energy from one food source. But an ecosystem is made of many organisms. These organisms form many food chains, and these food chains often overlap.

Tundra Ecosystem

8. Using the description of each organism in the tundra, write the role of each (producer, consumer, scavenger, decomposer) in the corresponding space in the diagram.

 **a. Caribou** eat reindeer moss and other producers to get the energy and matter they need.

 **b. Reindeer moss** uses energy from the sun to make matter in the form of sugars from air and water.

a. _____

b. _____

c. _____

d. _____

c. **Wolves** are predators. In the winter, they grow a second layer of fur for extra warmth. Animals such as caribou are their prey.

d. **Fungi and bacteria** do the cleanup work as they decompose the remains of tundra organisms.

e. Animals such as this **Arctic gull** feed on the dead bodies of other animals.

f. **Hawks** catch and eat prey that are smaller than they are, such as lemmings.

g. The **Arctic hare** mainly gets matter and energy from grasses and wildflowers.

h. **Grasses** are common in the diets of first-level consumers, such as the Arctic hare.

i. **Lemmings** are rodents that often live in Arctic ecosystems. They will eat any producer they can get their paws on!

j. **Arctic wildflowers** are producers. They are a favorite of first-level consumers in Arctic ecosystems.

e. _____

f. _____

g. _____

h. _____

i. _____

j. _____

Explore Online

Adding Connections to the Tundra

As you explored the tundra ecosystem on the previous pages, you probably noticed that organisms often eat more than one kind of food. One kind of producer may be food for more than one consumer. Also, some consumers, such as wolves, may eat different kinds of food.

A **food web** shows the relationships among different food chains. It shows how energy moves from producers to first- and higher-level consumers. The arrows point in the direction that energy moves.

Tundra Food Web

9. Use what you learned about the tundra ecosystem to draw or write the name of the organisms in the right spots on the food web.

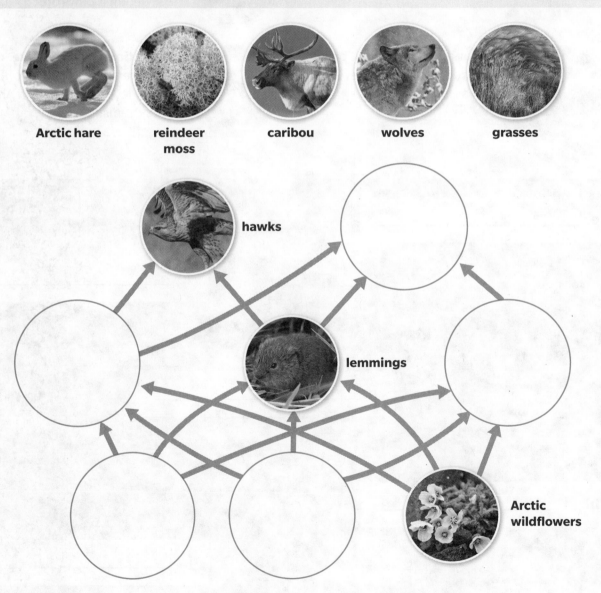

Arctic hare   reindeer moss   caribou   wolves   grasses

hawks

lemmings

Arctic wildflowers

Your food web shows how organisms in the tundra interact. Use the data from your tundra food web to describe these relationships. Circle "Yes" if the statement is true and "No" if the statement is not true.

10. Lemmings eat reindeer moss and Arctic hares.　　　　Yes　No

11. The following is a food chain within the tundra food web.　Yes　No

grasses　　**lemmings**　　**wolves**

12. If the lemmings were removed from the food web, the hawks would still have a source of food.　　　　Yes　No

13. Arctic hares and caribou are producers in the tundra.　　Yes　No

 **Explore Online**

In a food web, different populations are limited by different things. In addition to limiting factors, such as food, space, and water, predators may also limit population sizes. If the wolves were removed from this tundra food web, the caribou population would increase. More caribou would mean that more plants would be eaten. Eventually, other first-level consumers might run out of food and begin to die off. Losing just one component in an ecosystem can affect the other components.

 EVIDENCE NOTEBOOK Research other types of animals that are prey for owls. Think if or how these animals might help the owls to return. Write your evidence in your Evidence Notebook.

Putting it Together

14. Now that you know what food chains and food webs are, explain how they are related in an ecosystem. What would happen if there were an increase in the wolf population? Use your food web as evidence to support your answer.

_____

_____

_____

_____

_____

HANDS-ON ACTIVITY

Modeling Matter Moving within an Ecosystem

Objective

Collaborate with a partner to choose and model an ecosystem. Use this model to show how matter moves among organisms and their environment.

What question will you investigate to meet this objective?

_____

_____

_____

Materials
- materials to model
- scissors
- index cards
- markers
- paste
- string or yarn
- stapler

Procedure

STEP 1 With your partner, choose an ecosystem to model. Research the organisms you will include in your model ecosystem.

Which ecosystem are you researching?

_____

_____

Use your research to complete the table below.

Ecosystem	
Energy source	
Producers	Consumers
Decomposers	

STEP 2 Discuss with your partner how you want to model your ecosystem. For example, you could choose to make a diorama, create a poster, or design a digital model.

Describe how you will model your ecosystem.

_____

_____

_____

_____

STEP 3 Start by making the pieces of your system. Label each of your organisms as a producer, consumer, scavenger, or decomposer.

STEP 4 Arrange the organisms into food chains.

Based on your research, how do the organisms interact to move matter through the ecosystem?

_____

_____

_____

_____

STEP 5 Find the food chains that overlap. Connect the chains together. Your end result should look like a food web.

What is the relationship between food chains and food webs?

_____

_____

_____

_____

_____

Analyze Your Results

STEP 6 Compare your food web with those of other groups. How are they alike? How are they different?

_____

_____

_____

STEP 7 Predict what might happen if one of the organisms in your web disappeared. Remove one of the organisms from your web. Describe the results.

_____

_____

_____

Draw Conclusions

STEP 8 Is your food web a system? If so, what are the components in the food web?

_____

_____

_____

STEP 9 State a claim that is related to your question at the beginning of this activity.

_____

_____

Cite evidence from your food web to support your claim.

_____

_____

_____

STEP 10 Write another question you would like to ask about how matter moves through an ecosystem.

_____

_____

At the Top

Tracing Energy Flow

It takes a lot of producers to support a consumer at the top of a food chain. Although a high-level consumer probably doesn't eat the plants, the energy it uses comes from the producers at the bottom of the chain. But how much energy moves from one part of a food chain to the next?

Do the Math
Calculate Energy Units

15. **Arctic Wildflowers** The Arctic wildflowers in an area contain 2,000 units of energy.

The value **2,000** appears at the beginning of the food chain.

a. **Lemmings** The lemmings eat the Arctic wildflowers. But not all of the units of energy from Arctic wildflowers are available to the lemmings. Calculate the amount of energy that passes to the lemmings.

$$\boxed{2{,}000} \times \tfrac{1}{10} = \boxed{}$$

units produced by Arctic wildflowers — units that pass to lemmings

b. **Arctic Foxes** The Arctic foxes eat the lemmings. But not all of the units of energy from the lemmings are available to the Arctic foxes. Calculate the amount of energy that passes to the Arctic foxes.

$$\boxed{} \times \tfrac{1}{10} = \boxed{}$$

units received by lemmings — units that pass to Arctic foxes

c. **Wolves** The wolves eat the Arctic foxes. But not all of the units of energy from the Arctic foxes are available to the wolves. Calculate the amount of energy that passes to the wolves.

$$\boxed{} \times \tfrac{1}{10} = \boxed{}$$

units received by Arctic foxes — Units that pass to wolves

d. Now that you've determined the number of energy units available to each organism, add the correct values to the food chain.

Arctic wildflowers	lemming	Arctic fox	wolf
2,000			
energy units	energy units	energy units	energy units

235

A Closer Look at Energy Transfer

Not all the food energy of plants is passed on to the herbivores that eat them. Producers use about $\frac{9}{10}$ of the food energy they produce for their own life processes. They store the other $\frac{1}{10}$ in their leaves, stems, roots, fruits, and seeds. This means that animals that eat the producers get only $\frac{1}{10}$ of the energy the producers made. These herbivores then use $\frac{9}{10}$ of the energy they got from the producers for their life processes. They store the other $\frac{1}{10}$ in their bodies.

Tundra Energy Pyramid

16. Look at this food chain. Now write the name of each organism at the correct level of the energy pyramid.

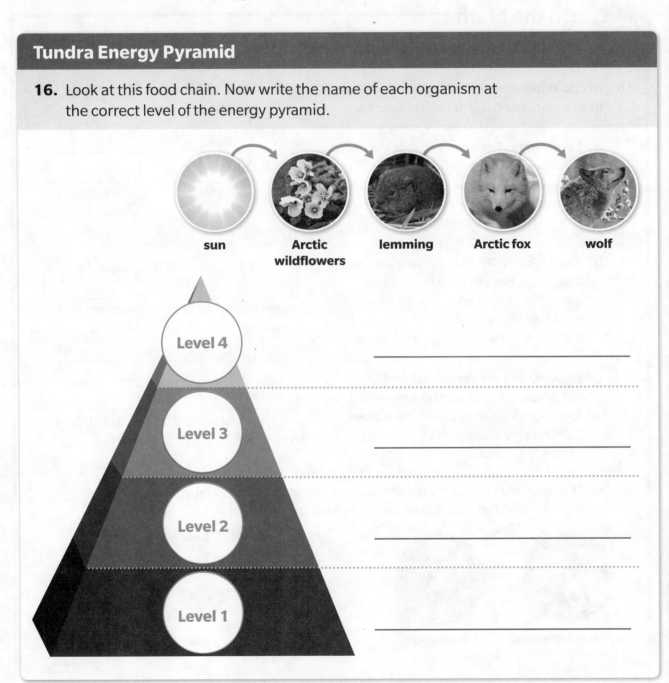

sun   Arctic wildflowers   lemming   Arctic fox   wolf

Level 4 _____

Level 3 _____

Level 2 _____

Level 1 _____

An **energy pyramid** shows how much energy passes from one organism to another up a food chain. Most of the energy in each level is used at that level. Only a little energy is passed to the next.

17. Language SmArts Each level in an ecosystem passes only a fraction of its available energy to the next level above. Compare the amount of producers to the amount of first-level consumers. Explain your reasoning.

_____

_____

_____

_____

As you can see, the producers make up the bottom level of the food pyramid. They have to be numerous in order to provide enough energy at the bottom levels to make it to the top. Lemmings are at the second level of the food chain because they are the first-level consumer in this food chain. The Arctic fox is on the third level of the energy pyramid, and the wolf is at the top.

18. Which of the following reasons explain why the wolf is at the top of this food pyramid?

  a. The wolf is the final consumer in this food chain.

  b. The wolf obtains most of its energy directly from producers.

  c. The wolf requires more energy than the lemming.

  d. The wolf has the largest population because it has the fewest sources of energy.

19. How does the lemming population size compare to the population size of the producers in this food chain?

  a. There are more lemmings than reindeer moss.

  b. There are fewer lemmings than reindeer moss.

  c. There are more wolves than lemmings.

  d. The populations are the same.

Picturing Energy Transfer

20. This energy pyramid represents the grasses-rabbits-owls ecosystem. Show the energy available to each population using a decimal square. Start with the grasses having 100 units of energy available.

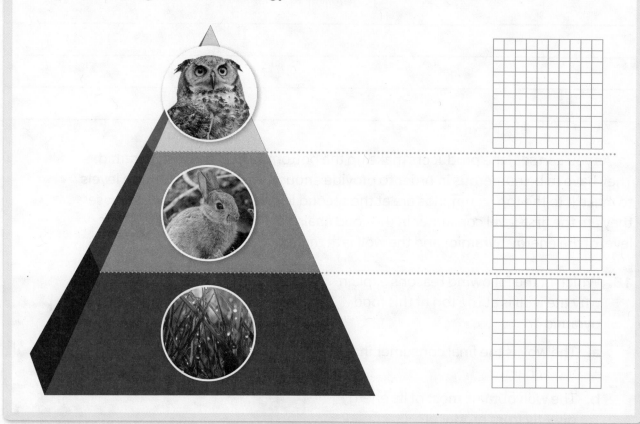

 EVIDENCE NOTEBOOK Examine the energy pyramid above. How would a disappearing rabbit population impact the owls' source of energy? Enter your observations in your Evidence Notebook.

Putting it Together

21. Now that you have learned about energy pyramids, explain why there are so many producers and first-level consumers.

_____

_____

_____

_____

Discover More

Check out this path . . . or go online to choose one of these other paths.

Careers in Science & Engineering

- **Exploring a Desert Ecosystem**
- **Exploring a Deep Sea Ecosystem**

Interview a Scientist

Explore Online

There are many kinds of scientists. Some scientists study ecosystems and how organisms interact. Read the interview below to learn more about a zoologist!

Person 1: A career as a zoologist sounds interesting. Does a zoologist work at a zoo?

Person 2: A zoologist is a scientist who studies animals. Some zoologists do work at zoos, but there are many other places zoologists can work.

Person 1: Can you give me some examples?

Person 2: Sure! Some zoologists work in labs doing research. Other zoologists, like me, work in ecosystems around the world, observing animals in their natural habitats.

Person 1: Did you have to go to college to become a zoologist?

Person 2: Yes. I went to college and earned a degree in zoology. I learned about many different areas of research.

Person 1: Tell me about some of the projects you have done as part of your job.

Person 2: One of my favorite projects was working with an endangered species. I helped to study the species' habitat and worked on a recovery plan to help save the species from extinction. Another interesting project was finding out about the effects of pollution from a factory on fish species in a river.

22. Now that you know what zoologists do, collaborate with one or more classmates to select a few careers where scientists research how organisms interact in food webs. Each group member should choose a different career to learn about and report back to the group. Then, as a group, decide on which career you want to share with the class. Use the box below to write interview questions and answers in the format of a script. When you've completed all your questions and answers, present the information to your class as an interview.

Tip

If you're stuck, some examples of careers related to animal interactions include primatologist, wildlife biologist, entomologist, and cetologist.

Lesson Check

Name _____

Can You Explain It?

1. Now that you've learned more about food chains, explain what has happened to the owls. Be sure to do the following:

   • Identify what has happened to the owls' ecosystem.

   • Describe why the changes have caused the owls to leave.

   • Identify what the city can do to try to get the owls to come back.

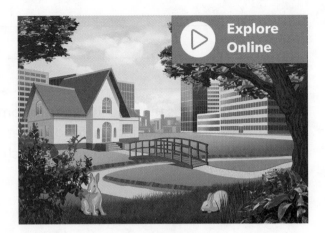

Explore Online

 EVIDENCE NOTEBOOK Use the information you've collected in your Evidence Notebook to help you cover each point.

_____

_____

_____

_____

_____

_____

_____

Checkpoints

2. Put these items in the correct order to make a food chain.

hawk

sun

corn

mouse

_____ → _____ → _____ → _____

3. A disease has killed many trees in an ecosystem. What do you think will happen to the organisms in the area?

_____

_____

_____

4. Many food chains that use the energy from the sun are involved in producing the food we eat. Use the terms in the box to complete each food chain below.

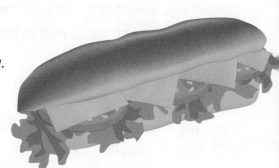

tomato	grass	sun
you	cow	lettuce

a. _____ sun _____ → _____ → _____

b. _____ → _____ → _____

c. _____ → _____ → _____ → _____ you _____

Use the food chain to answer 5 and 6.

sun   grasses   grasshoppers   frogs   snakes

5. The _____ use $\frac{9}{10}$ of the energy and matter they make and pass

on $\frac{1}{10}$ to the grasshoppers that eat them.

6. Which organism is the most plentiful in this food chain?
  a. grasses   **c.** frogs
  b. grasshoppers   **d.** snakes

Lesson Roundup

Use these options to answer the questions below.

sun   hawk   lemming   Arctic wildflower

A. Write the correct name of each organism in each box below to show how energy and matter move through the food chain.

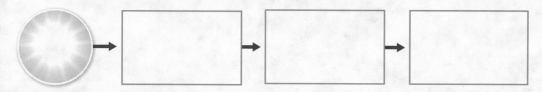

B. Complete the food web by writing the names of the missing organisms in the boxes.

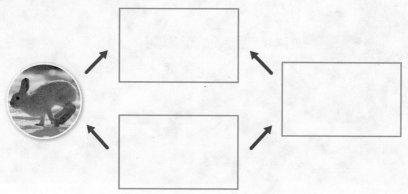

C. Write the name of the organism that belongs at each level of the energy pyramid, and predict the units of energy available.

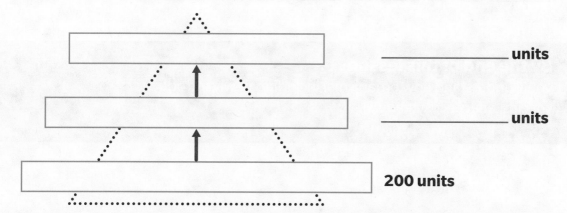

_____ **units**

_____ **units**

200 units

243

How Do Organisms Change Their Ecosystems?

The lionfish, which occurs naturally in the Pacific Ocean, was introduced to the Atlantic Ocean. Lionfish eat many kinds of fish and are disrupting marine ecosystems around Florida.

By the end of this lesson . . .
you'll understand how organisms, including newly introduced species, affect ecosystems.

Can You Explain It?

 Explore Online

Burmese pythons are taking over the Florida Everglades. Burmese pythons are originally from Asia but are rapidly increasing in numbers despite attempts to control their population.

1. How do you think pythons were first introduced into the ecosystem in Florida? Why is the population growing so quickly? How do you think the python problem could be fixed?

Tip

Learn more about how organisms interact with each other in *How Do Organisms Interact?*

_____

_____

_____

_____

_____

_____

_____

 EVIDENCE NOTEBOOK Look for this icon to help you gather evidence to answer the question above.

245

Redecorating Environments

Organisms' Effects

All living things interact with the living and nonliving parts of their ecosystems. When living things interact with other components of their ecosystems and environments, they cause different kinds of effects.

These beavers are building a dam. First, they knock down trees by gnawing on their trunks. Then, they use the logs and branches to build the dam. The dam slows the flow of water. This keeps the entrance to the beavers' home underwater, helping the beavers stay safe from predators.

2. How does the dam affect the living and nonliving parts of this ecosystem?

_____

_____

_____

3. What are changes that other animals you know of make to their habitats or ecosystems?

_____

_____

Diverse Effects

Beavers building a dam is one example of a way that living things affect the environment. What are some other examples of effects?

These giant ant hills have thousands or millions of ants. Ants build their hills by moving soil, mud, or plant matter. The changes to the ant's ecosystem are not only above ground. Ant colonies' tunnels extend below ground as well.

Woodpeckers may make small changes that affect living parts of their environment—trees. Woodpeckers use their bills to peck through tree bark to get at the insects inside. Sometimes this exposes the inner parts of the tree.

Corals affect their environment by forming the foundation of reefs. As coral grows and dies, the structure grows larger. If reefs are thrust upward by events on the ocean floor, or if sea levels fall, reefs can become islands.

Plants carry out photosynthesis, absorbing carbon dioxide from the atmosphere and releasing oxygen. Plant roots affect the soil they grow in. As roots grow and change shape, they can move soil and break rock.

4. Select two of the ecosystem effects shown in the images. Explain how the pictured effect could affect two other living things in the ecosystem that aren't in the picture. Include specific details in your response.

_____

_____

_____

_____

We Cause Changes

Like all animals, humans affect their environments. Humans cause changes when they build places to live, work, and go to school. Humans also change the environment when they grow food and make products. Pollution occurs when human processes release wastes that affect the land, air, or water.

Many cities contain homes, offices, roads, and schools. Construction of these structures causes major changes to the environment.

Pollution caused by humans affects the environment. It often needs to be cleaned up to reduce damage. This person is attempting to clean a bird that was affected by an oil spill.

Chemicals and waste products can affect an ecosystem when they are released. Some directly harm living things. Others may result in population booms of bacteria that make life more difficult for other organisms.

When humans cut down trees to build homes, roads, and farms, the environment changes. Humans can also plant trees to replace trees that were cut down.

5. List two other ways humans affect the environment.

_____

_____

_____

Engineer It!
Clean It Up!

6. Work with a partner. Research ways that humans may damage the environment and ways humans attempt to reduce the damage afterwards. Choose one type of change caused by humans. Using your findings, design a machine that will reduce human impacts on the environment or will clean up damage. Make sure you consider the following in your design:

- What type of human impact will you attempt to reduce or clean up?
- What are your constraints?
- How would you observe and measure how well your design works?

When you are done, present your findings and your design to the class.

7. Language SmArts You have learned that effects in ecosystems can be caused by many different kinds of living things. Think about the interactions between decomposers and other kinds of living things. In what ways do decomposers affect the environment? What do you think would happen if all decomposers disappeared from an ecosystem?

_____

_____

_____

_____

EVIDENCE NOTEBOOK You've learned how living things affect their environment. In your Evidence Notebook, describe how Burmese pythons might be changing the Everglades ecosystem.

Putting It Together

8. Describe a specific example that demonstrates how a plant or an animal can affect its environment.

_____

_____

_____

_____

_____

Introduced and Invasive Species

New in Town

Sometimes species get introduced into an ecosystem they have never before been a part of. These species can cause big changes to the ecosystem.

Explore Online

Kudzu is native to Asia, where its population is controlled by insects. It was introduced to the United States more than 100 years ago, and has since become known as "the plant that ate the south."

Kudzu vines can grow 30 centimeters per day. In an attempt to control it, kudzu is sometimes burned. Kudzu can also be pulled out or grazing animals can be brought in to eat it.

Newly introduced species, also known as non-native species, can cause changes in ecosystems. In many cases, newly introduced species do not survive well in their new ecosystem. They might not find the right food, or the physical conditions of the ecosystem might not allow them to survive.

Sometimes, though, introduced species can thrive and take over an ecosystem. An **invasive species** is an introduced species that is better able to compete for resources than the existing species in the ecosystem. The existing, or native, species might not be able to get what they need to survive. Invasive species can spread rapidly, causing native species to die out.

Losing Balance

The images below show other kinds of plants that have invaded new ecosystems and caused damage.

The water chestnut is an aquatic plant introduced to ecosystems in the United States more than 100 years ago. Its leaves spread on the surface of water, blocking sunlight needed by other species in the ecosystem.

Brazilian elodea is an invasive aquatic plant that was introduced into the United States more than 100 years ago. It is available for sale for use in aquariums. Elodea grows into dense mat-like structures that block sunlight from other plants.

Garlic mustard, native to Europe, was brought to the United States in the late 1800s for use as medicine and food. It uses up resources needed by native forest species. Because few animal species eat this plant, it is hard to control.

Japanese honeysuckle is native to East Asia. It was brought to the United States in the late 1800s for use as a garden plant. This invasive vine grows in field and forests. Like kudzu, it climbs, covers, and crowds out other plants.

9. Choose the correct words to complete each sentence.

crowd out	increase	decrease	will	will not

Invasive plants affect ecosystems in many ways. They can _____

native plants. The food supply for existing first-level consumers will

_____. Second- and third-level consumers _____

be affected.

Animal Invasion

Animals can also be invasive species. Unlike plants, they do not usually smother other species, but they can cause a lot of damage.

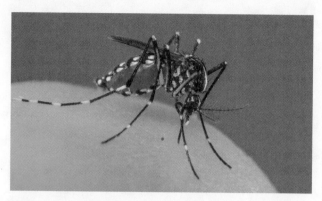

The Asian tiger mosquito arrived in the mainland part of the United States in 1985. It is a carrier for several human and animal diseases.

Tegu lizards were probably released as pets. These lizards are invasive in Florida where they compete with native species for resources.

European starlings were introduced to the United States in the 1890s. Flocks of starlings consume huge amounts of food. They often destroy the nests of other bird species.

Several invasive species of Asian carp are causing major changes in plant and animal populations in the United States. They compete with native species for food, and native predators aren't able to control the carp populations.

Nutria were introduced to the United States from South America for fur production. They damage the wetlands and marshes by destroying vegetation.

The cane toad, native to South and Central America was introduced in Australia to eat pests on sugar cane. But they also eat foods needed by native species, and this kills predators.

Invasive animals can be harder to control than some invasive plants because the animals are mobile. In environments where they can easily camouflage themselves, they can be hard to track even if they are relatively large, such as the Burmese python.

10. How do invasive animal populations affect ecosystems? Choose all that apply.

a. They use food sources needed by native species.

b. They add resources, such as space and water, to existing ecosystems.

c. They change existing food chains and food webs.

d. They block sunlight needed by native plant species.

Do the Math
Pig Populations

Wild pigs are an invasive species causing big problems in some parts of the United States. They eat almost anything, and they destroy vegetation as they trample over it. They don't have any predators in their new ecosystems. And the pig population is growing fast!

A female wild pig can reproduce about ten times in her lifetime. Each time she reproduces, she has an average of six offspring.

11. Using the information given, how many offspring can a female wild pig produce in her lifetime? _____. This is the number of pigs in the second generation.

12. If half of the pigs in the second generation are female, how many offspring could those female pigs produce? _____. The offspring produced are the third generation.

13. If half of the pigs in the third generation are female, how many offspring could they produce in their lifetime? _____. The offspring produced are the fourth generation.

14. If half of the fourth generation is female, how many pigs do you think would be in the fifth generation? _____.

Engineer It!
Toad Trap

The cane toad is an invasive species that can damage the balance of ecosystems. Scientists have tried to develop ways to eradicate the cane toad populations.

15. Research cane toads to learn more about their behavior, their characteristics, and what they need to survive. Use what you have learned to design a device to catch cane toads. The trap should be designed with the cane toad's specific characteristics in mind and should include features that will help prevent the trap from capturing other animals. Make a sketch below, and write a description of your design. Submit your design to your teacher.

Language SmArts
Unwelcome Guests

16. You have learned that invasive species damage the balance in ecosystems. Select one invasive species, and write a scientific explanation of specific ways in which this species causes changes in the ecosystem.

_____

_____

_____

_____

_____

HANDS-ON ACTIVITY
Invasion!

Objective

Collaborate with a group to model how invasive species, such as the northern snakehead, can affect the food supply of an area.

What question will you investigate to meet this objective?

_____

_____

Materials
- index cards (4)
- small squares of construction paper (10 squares each of red, blue, and yellow paper)
- paper clips

Consider This Invasive species damage the balance in ecosystems by disrupting native species and using resources. The northern snakehead is an invasive species. It is native to Korea, China, and Russia. It was first found in the United States in 1997. Adult northern snakeheads eat other fish and insects.

In what ways could a northern snakehead damage the balance in an ecosystem?

_____

Procedure

STEP 1 With your group, research three fish species found in U.S. ecosystems affected by northern snakeheads. Write the name of these species or draw each of them on their own index card. On the fourth card, draw a northern snakehead. Place a paper clip on each card.

How do you think the northern snakehead could affect the other fish species?

_____

_____

STEP 2 Set out the ecosystem's food supply on the table in front of your group. Fill out the table with the species you have selected. For this activity, you can place any of the species in any of the rows. Use the colored construction paper squares to represent food for the native species.

Native species	Food requirement (one round)
	3 blue squares, 2 red squares
	3 yellow squares
	3 red squares, 1 blue square

STEP 3 Allow the native fish in the ecosystem to feed by placing the required amount of food squares (based on the information in the table) into the paper clips on the index cards.

Is the ecosystem in balance? Why or why not?

_____

_____

_____

_____

Which two native species appear to compete the most for food?

_____

_____

_____

STEP 4 After the first round of feeding, the northern snakehead is introduced into the ecosystem. The snakehead can outcompete the native species for food. To model this, the snakehead gets to eat first. The snakehead eats the following: 2 yellow squares, 4 red squares, and 3 blue squares.

Record the food remaining after Round 1 in the table below, then proceed with the second round of feeding, first with the snakehead eating what it needs, then all of the other species trying to meet their own needs. Use the table to keep track of how much food is left after each round and whether each species has survived.

Did the snakehead change the ecosystem? How?

_____

_____

_____

Round	Red food remaining	Blue food remaining	Yellow food remaining	Result to native species
1				
2				
3				

Analyze Your Results

STEP 5 Which fish species did not have enough to eat in the second round? Would those species have had enough to eat without the snakehead?

_____

_____

_____

STEP 6 Compare your results to the results of other groups. Describe any similarities or differences you notice.

_____

_____

_____

Draw Conclusions

STEP 7 In this activity, you observed how an invasive species changed an ecosystem by modeling how it affected the food webs in the ecosystem. How do you think your results would be similar or different if you modeled a different way in which northern snakeheads affect ecosystems?

_____

_____

_____

STEP 8 Did your model provide evidence supporting the argument that an invasive species damages the balance in an ecosystem? Explain.

_____

_____

_____

STEP 9 How could this activity be made more realistic in terms of the availability of food for the native species and the invasive species? Explain.

_____

_____

_____

STEP 10 What other questions do you have about the ways in which introduced and invasive species can change ecosystems?

_____

_____

_____

Discover More

Check out this path . . . or go online to choose one of these other paths.

Careers in Science & Engineering

- It's News to Me!
- Fantastic Field Guides

U.S. Army Corps of Engineers

Explore Online

The U.S. Army Corps of Engineers carries out many kinds of projects. It helps build and maintain some buildings, develops new technologies, maintains waterways, and helps when a natural disaster strikes.

Invasive plants affect both land and water ecosystems. They can disrupt the balance in ecosystems by crowding out native plants. This scientist is identifying this leaf by smelling it.

Another major role of the U.S. Army Corps of Engineers is conserving and protecting ecosystems from invasive species. The Corps uses a wide variety of methods and technologies to control invasive species. These methods include biological, mechanical, and chemical control methods. Managing invasive species is one of the major ways in which the Army Corps of Engineers protects the nation's ecosystems.

17. Research an invasive aquatic species. Using what you learn, propose two possible methods of controlling the species. At least one of the methods should be mechanical. This means that it should use a device or structure to control the invasive species.

Write a description of each of your proposed methods. Include a comparison of your proposed methods to methods of control that have already been tried. Then draw a diagram or build a model of one of your proposed methods. Explain how the method would be applied, how it would work, and the materials required to construct it.

Turn in your completed model and explanation to the teacher.

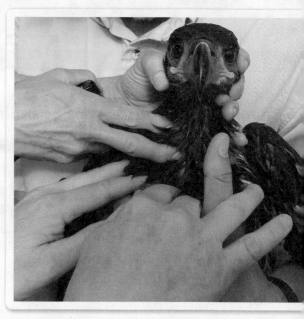

In addition to controlling invasive species, the U.S. Army Corp also takes care of native species.

Lesson Check

Name _____

Can You Explain It?

Explore Online

1. You've learned about ways organisms affect their environments. Now explain how the Burmese Python is affecting the Everglades. Be sure to do the following:

- Describe how Burmese pythons were probably introduced and could damage the balance in the ecosystem.

- Explain methods you could use to control the python population.

- State why your solution would effectively control the Burmese python population without causing harm to other species.

> **EVIDENCE NOTEBOOK** Use the information you've collected in your Evidence Notebook to help you cover each point above.

_____

_____

_____

_____

_____

_____

_____

Checkpoints

2. How do the animals in the photograph affect their ecosystem? Choose all that apply.

   a. They use trees that other organisms might need for shelter.

   b. They build dams that change the flow of streams and rivers.

   c. They block sunlight needed by native plant species.

   d. They use up the supply of oxygen in the water.

3. Which of the following is not a way that trees affect their ecosystems?

   a. reducing the number of insects by eating them

   b. moving soil as root growth occurs

   c. releasing oxygen into the atmosphere

   d. absorbing water from the soil

4. Match each living thing to the description of how it affects the environment.

| humans | squirrels | woodpeckers | coral |

Type of Living Thing	How It Affects the Environment
	Make holes in tree trunks to capture insects for food .
	Life cycle results in growth of reef structure, which provides food and habitat for many types of organisms.
	Changes existing ecosystems by building roads, schools, and homes.
	Move and store nuts, leading to trees growing in new locations.

5. Which of these describe(s) an invasive species? Choose all that apply.

   a. better able to compete for resources than native species

   b. any species that is added to a new ecosystem

   c. usually dies out rapidly in its new ecosystem

   d. tends to spread rapidly and take over ecosystems

   e. usually lacks predators in the new ecosystem

6. Which of these describe(s) how this invasive species, Brazilian elodea, affects other plants in the ecosystems it enters? Choose all that apply.

   a. It crowds out other plants.

   b. It produces resources needed by other plants.

   c. It increases the number of native plants in the ecosystem.

   d. It blocks sunlight from plants that live deeper in the water.

Lesson Roundup

A. Label the effects on ecosystems as being caused by plants, animals, or both.

_____ moving soil as roots grow, moving materials to build homes

_____ using water resources

_____ adding and removing materials from the air

B. Describe one way organisms change their ecosystem.

_____

_____

_____

C. Choose the correct words to complete each sentence.

| introduced | native | invasive | is | is not |

Species that are newly added to an ecosystem are called

_____ species. If a newly added species can

better compete than the species that were already part of the

ecosystem, it could become an _____ species.

Adding a new species to an ecosystem to control another species

is usually _____ the best solution.

D. Write *native* or *invasive* before each description that describes the species.

_____ is established in an ecosystem

_____ upsets the balance in an ecosystem

_____ may have population explosions

_____ is better able than other species to compete for resources

in an ecosystem

ENGINEER IT!

Design an Ecosystem

You work for a company that is builds terrariums and habitats for animals. After studying the animals' natural ecosystems, your team needs to choose an animal to design the habitat for. Your team has access to an empty room with a sprinkler for precipitation and temperature control. There are skylights in the ceiling to allow sunlight in. The ground is covered in soil.

This reptile terrarium has everything the lizard needs to survive.

FIND A PROBLEM: What problem do you need to solve?

_____

_____

_____

Before beginning, look at the checklist at the end of this project to be sure you are meeting all the requirements.

RESEARCH: Study the animal you plan to bring to the habitat, and write down your observations. Use online or library resources for research. Use multiple sources, and cite them.

_____

_____

BRAINSTORM: Brainstorm three or more ideas with your team to solve the problem. Keep in mind the criteria and constraints.

Criteria	Constraints
☐ Animal must survive.	☐ Your animal will not have access to the natural outdoors.
☐ The landscape must mimic the animal's natural ecosystem.	☐ Limited to one room to build your ecosystem.
☐ A food web must be present to meet your animal's nutrition needs.	☐ Room is about the size of your classroom.
☐ The animal needs enough room to exercise and move freely.	☐ Ceiling height is 3 meters.

MAKE A PLAN: Make a plan by considering the questions below. Answer the questions and make a list of needed materials and why you need them.

1. What supplies will you need and why?

2. Describe your habitat in terms of the climate, landforms, and natural resources you will need to make.

3. Create a food web for your ecosystem. Include producers, consumers, scavengers, and decomposers.

This girl is making a sketch of her ecosystem.

_____

_____

_____

_____

_____

_____

BUILD: Make a model of your ecosystem. Label all living and nonliving items. It can be a paper model, a digital model, or even a 3D model.

EVALUATE AND REDESIGN: Did you meet the criteria and constraints? What are the ways you could improve your design? Make changes to your model to improve it.

COMMUNICATE: Present your ecosystem to your class using multimedia resources.

Checklist

Review your project and check off each completed item.

_____ Includes a list of what is included in your ecosystem and the reasons why they are needed. Multiple sources are cited.

_____ Includes a description of your ecosystem.

_____ Includes a labeled food web.

_____ Includes a list of potential problems with solutions.

_____ A sketch of your ecosystem was produced.

_____ Ecosystem was presented using multimedia.

Unit Review

Use this image to answer questions 1 and 2.

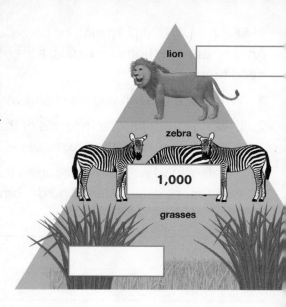

1. Trace the flow of energy through the food pyramid. Label the missing units of energy found at each level by calculating the change in energy.

2. What is the original source of energy for this food pyramid?

   a. grasses   **b.** lion   **c.** sun   **d.** zebra

3. What is true of invasive species? Select all that apply.

   a. They are typically harmful to their new environment.

   b. They can limit resources available to other plants.

   c. They are often eaten by native animal species.

   d. They typically spread very slowly.

   e. They are native to an area.

4. Write the names of the parts of the ecosystem into the food chain in the correct order.

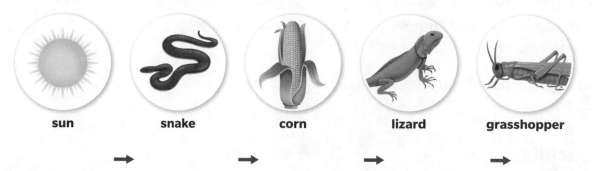

| **sun** | **snake** | **corn** | **lizard** | **grasshopper** |

_____ → _____ → _____ → _____ → _____

5. José was researching carrion beetles and he found the following information: Carrion beetles crawl inside dead animals and eat them. They lay their eggs near a dead animal so that the larvae can eat the dead animal after hatching. Using this evidence, pick the claim he should state for the report he is writing.

   a. The carrion beetle is a scavenger.

   b. The carrion beetle is a producer.

   c. The carrion beetle is a decomposer.

   d. The carrion beetle is an invasive species.

Use this image to answer questions 6 and 7.

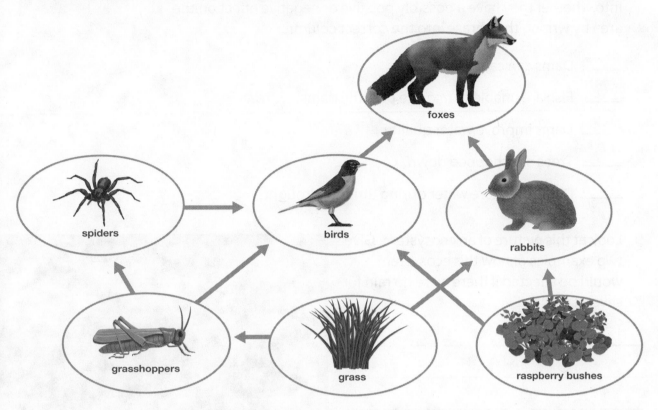

6. How does the energy and food matter move from the raspberry bushes to the fox in this food web?

   a. The rabbit eats the raspberry bushes, the bird eats the rabbit, and the fox eats the bird.

   b. The grasshopper eats the raspberry bushes, the rabbit eats the grasshopper, and the fox eats the rabbit.

   c. The bird eats the raspberry bushes, and the fox eats the bird.

   d. The spider eats the grasses, the grasshopper eats the spider, the bird eats the grasshopper, and the fox eats the bird.

7. In the food web shown, the raspberry bushes and grasses are producers. What is true of the raspberry bushes and grasses? Select all that apply.

   a. They can make their own food.

   b. They use energy from the sun to make food.

   c. They get energy from other plants and animals.

   d. They decompose the remains of plants and animals for food.

8. Categorize the series of events created by beavers in an ecosystem into whether they have a possibly positive or negative effect on the area by writing the phrase into the correct column.

_____ Dams can cause flooding.

_____ Fish are unable to migrate past the dams.

_____ Dams improve water quality.

_____ Trees are chopped down.

_____ Dams can store water during times of drought.

9. Look at this picture of an ecosystem. Give two examples of how this ecosystem would be affected if there were no rain for several months.

_____

_____

_____

_____

_____

_____

10. Zebra mussels are tiny animals that attach themselves to things in water. A female zebra mussel can produce up to 500,000 eggs at a time. These animals can cause quite a few problems in the waters they inhabit. Below are some issues caused by zebra mussels.

• They attach themselves to native mussels and smother them.

• They attach themselves to boat motors and make the motors stop working.

• They eat tiny food particles that native organisms usually consume.

What are two things people can do to stop the spread of zebra mussels?

_____

_____

_____

Interactive Glossary

As you learn about each item, add notes, drawings, or sentences in the extra space. This will help you remember what the terms mean. Here is an example:

fungi (FUHN•jee) A group of organisms that get nutrients by decomposing other organisms

hongos Un grupo de organismos que obtienen sus nutrientes al descomponer otros organismos.

Mushrooms are a type of fungi.

Glossary Pronunciation Key

With every glossary term, there is also a phonetic respelling. A phonetic respelling writes the word the way it sounds, which can help you pronounce new or unfamiliar words. Use this key to help you understand the respellings.

Sound	As in	Phonetic Respelling	Sound	As in	Phonetic Respelling
a	bat	(BAT)	oh	over	(OH•ver)
ah	lock	(LAHK)	oo	pool	(POOL)
air	rare	(RAIR)	ow	out	(OWT)
ar	argue	(AR•gyoo)	oy	foil	(FOYL)
aw	law	(LAW)	s	cell	(SEL)
ay	face	(FAYS)		sit	(SIT)
ch	chapel	(CHAP•uhl)	sh	sheep	(SHEEP)
e	test	(TEST)	th	that	(THAT)
	metric	(MEH•trik)		thin	(THIN)
ee	eat	(EET)	u	pull	(PUL)
	feet	(FEET)	uh	medal	(MED•uhl)
	ski	(SKEE)		talent	(TAL•uhnt)
er	paper	(PAY•per)		pencil	(PEN•suhl)
	fern	(FERN)		onion	(UHN•yuhn)
eye	idea	(eye•DEE•uh)		playful	(PLAY•fuhl)
i	bit	(BIT)		dull	(DUHL)
ing	going	(GOH•ing)	y	yes	(YES)
k	card	(KARD)		ripe	(RYP)
	kite	(KYT)	z	bags	(BAGZ)
ngk	bank	(BANGK)	zh	treasure	(TREZH•er)

A

atmosphere (AT•muhs•feer) The mixture of gases that surround a planet. p. 368

atmósfera Combinación de los gases que rodean el planeta.

axis (AK•sis) The imaginary line around which Earth rotates. p. 297

eje Línea imaginaria en torno a la cual rota la Tierra.

B

biodegradable [by•oh•dee•GRA•duh•buhl] Able to be decomposed by living organisms. p. 480

biodegradable Que puede ser descompuesto por organismos vivos.

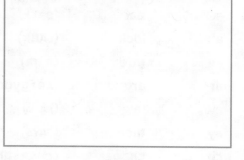

biosphere (BY•oh•sfeer) All the living things on Earth. p. 368

biósfera Conjunto de todos los seres vivos de la Tierra.

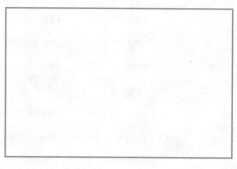

boiling point (BOYL•ing POINT) The point at which matter changes from a liquid to a gas. p. 132

punto de ebullición Punto en el que la materia cambia de líquido a gas.

brainstorming (BRAYN•storm•ing) Collecting as many ideas as you can, however good you think they are. p. 32

lluvia de ideas Recopilación de la mayor cantidad de ideas posible, sin importar el valor que creas que puedan tener.

chemical change (KEM•ih•kuhl CHAYNJ) Change in one or more substance, caused by a reaction, that forms new and different substances. p. 136

cambio químico Cambio en una sustancia o más, causado por una reacción que genera sustancias nuevas y distintas.

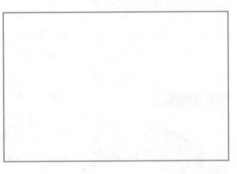

C

coastline (KOST•lyn) The place at which land masses meet the ocean. p. 420

costa Lugar en el que las masas terrestres se encuentran con el océano.

C

community

(kuh•MYOO•nih•tee) A group of organisms that live in the same area and interact with one another. p. 205

comunidad Grupo de organismos que viven en la misma área e interactúan entre sí.

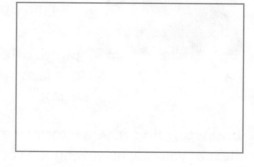

condensation

(kahn•duhn•SAY•shuhn) The process by which a gas changes into a liquid. p. 391

condensación Proceso por el cual un gas se convierte en líquido.

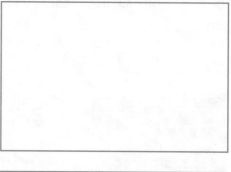

conservation of matter

(kahn•ser•VAY•shuhn uhv MAT•ur) A law that states that matter cannot be made or destroyed; however, matter can change into a new form. p. 143

conservación de la materia Ley que establece que la materia no se crea ni se destruye, sino que se transforma en algo nuevo.

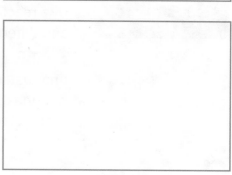

conserve (kuhn•SERV) To preserve and protect an ecosystem or a resource. p. 448

conservar Preservar y proteger un ecosistema o recurso.

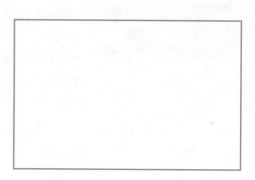

constellation
(kon•stuh•LEY•shuhn) A pattern of stars that form an imaginary picture or design in the sky. p. 296

constelación Patrón de estrellas que forman un diseño o dibujo imaginario en el cielo.

constraint (KUHN•straint) Something that limits the solution you are designing. p. 28

restricción Algo que limita la solución que se está diseñando.

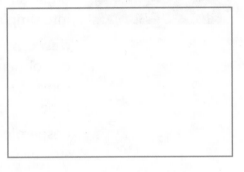

consumer (kuhn•SOOM•er) A living thing that cannot make its own food and must eat other living things. p. 182

consumidor Ser vivo que no puede producir su propio alimento y por eso debe alimentarse de otros seres vivos.

criteria (kry•TEER•ee•uh) The desirable features of a solution. p. 28

criterios Características deseables para una solución.

D

decompose (dee•kuhm•POHZ) Breaking down dead organisms and animal wastes into simpler substances to get energy. p. 471

descomponer Romper, separar o desbaratar organismos muertos y desperdicios animales en sustancias más simples para obtener energía.

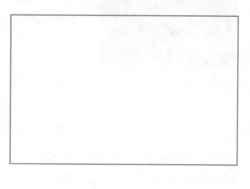

decomposer (dee•kuhm•POHZ•er) A living thing that gets energy by breaking down dead organisms and animal wastes into simpler substances. p. 227

descomponedor Ser vivo que obtiene su energía al romper, separar o desbaratar organismos muertos y

desperdicios animales en sustancias más simples.

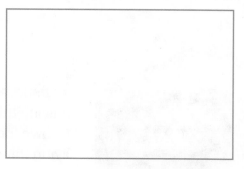

deforestation (de•FOR•is•ta•shuhn) The process of cutting down trees to plant crops. p. 41

deforestación Acción de cortar y eliminar árboles para el cultivo.

E

ecosystem (EE•koh•sis•tuhm) A community of organisms and the environment in which they live. p.198

ecosistema Comunidad de organismos y ambiente en el que viven.

energy pyramid (EN•er•jee PIR•uh•mid) A diagram that shows that energy is lost at each level in a food chain. p. 237

pirámide de energía Diagrama que muestra que se pierde energía en cada nivel de la cadena alimentaria.

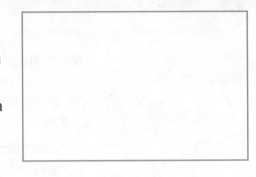

environment (en•VY•ruhn•muhnt) All of the living and nonliving things that surround and affect an organism. p. 198

medio ambiente Todo los seres vivos y no vivos que rodean y afectan a un organismo.

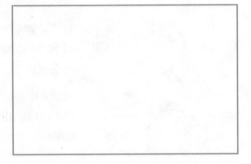

erosion (uh•ROH•zhuhn) The process of moving sediment from one place to another. p. 30

erosión Acción de mover sedimento de un lugar a otro.

evaporation (ee•VAP•uh•ray•shuhn) The process by which a liquid changes into a gas. p. 391

evaporación Proceso por el cual un líquido se transforma en gas.

F

food chain (FOOD CHAYN) The transfer of food energy between organisms in an ecosystem. p. 226

cadena alimentaria Transferencia de energía alimentaria entre organismos en un ecosistema.

food web (FOOD WEB) A group of food chains that overlap. p. 230

red alimentaria Grupo de cadenas alimentarias que se superponen.

freezing point (FREE•zing POINT) The temperature at which matter changes from a liquid to a solid. p. 130

punto de congelación Temperatura en la que la materia cambia de líquida a sólida.

G

geosphere (JEE•o•sfeer) The solid portion of Earth. p. 369

geósfera La parte sólida de la Tierra.

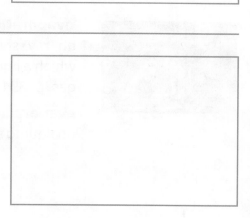

gravity (GRAV•ih•tee) A force that pulls things toward the center of the Earth. p. 283

gravedad Fuerza que atrae los objetos hacia el centro de la Tierra.

H

habitat (HAB•ih•tat) The place where an organism lives and can find everything it needs to survive. p. 200

hábitat Lugar donde vive un organismo y donde puede encontrar todo lo necesario para sobrevivir.

hemisphere (HEM•i•sfeer) One half of Earth. p. 284

hemisferio Una mitad de la Tierra.

hydrosphere (HI•dro•sfeer) All of Earth's water, taken together in all states of matter. p. 369

hidrósfera Toda el agua de la Tierra, junta y en cualquier estado de la materia.

I

invasive species (in•VAY•siv SPEE•sheez) An organism that is nonnative to an environment and disrupts the stable web of life. p. 250

especies invasivas Organismo que no es nativo de un ambiente y altera la red estable de la vida.

M

matter (MAT•er) Anything that has mass and takes up space. p. 78

materia Cualquier cosa que tiene masa y ocupa espacio.

melting point (MEL•ting point) The temperature at which matter is changed from a solid p. 131

punto de fusión Temperatura en la cual la materia cambia de sólido a líquido.

mixture (MIKS•cher) A combination of two or more different substances in which the substances keep their identities. p. 114

mezcla Combinación de dos o más sustancias diferentes en la que estas mantienen sus identidades.

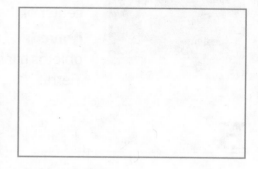

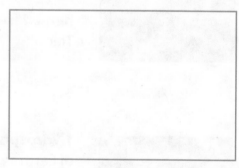

N

natural resource (NACH•er•uhl REE•sawrs) Anything from nature that people can use. p. 448

recurso natural Todo lo que provenga de la naturaleza y que las personas puedan usar.

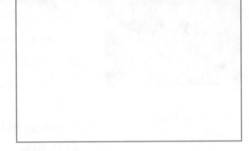

niche (NICH) The role that a plant or animal plays in its habitat. p. 200

nicho Rol que juega una planta o un animal en su hábitat.

O

orbit (AWR•bit) The path of one object in space around another object. p. 314

órbita La trayectoria de un objeto alrededor de otro en el espacio.

P

photosynthesis (foh•toh•SIN•thuh•sis) The process that plants use to make sugar. p.170

fotosíntesis Proceso en el cual las plantas generan azúcar.

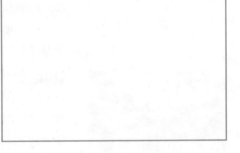

physical change (FIZ•ih•kuhl CHAYNJ) A change in which the shape or form of the substance changes but the substance still has the same physical makeup. p. 128

cambio físico Transformación en la que cambia el estado o la forma de una sustancia pero esta se mantiene con la misma composición física.

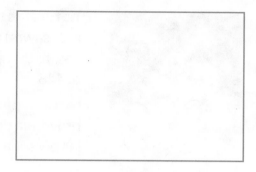

physical properties (FIZ•ih•kuhl PRAHP•er•tees) Anything that you can observe about an object by using one or more of your senses. p. 106

propiedad física Todo lo que se pueda observar de un objeto usando uno o más sentidos.

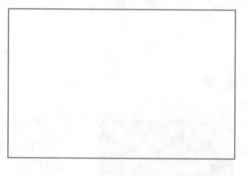

pollution (puh•LOO•shuhn) Any waste product or contamination that harms or dirties an ecosystem and harms organisms. p. 449

contaminación Todo desperdicio que daña o ensucia un ecosistema y hace daño a sus organismos.

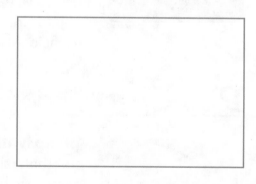

population (pahp•yuh•LAY•shuhn) All the organisms of the same kind that live together in a given area. pp. 205, 452

población Todos los organismos del mismo tipo que viven juntos en un ecosistema.

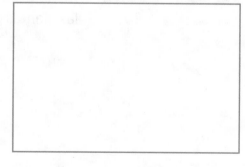

precipitation (pree•sip•uh•TAY•shuhn) Water that falls from the air to Earth's surface. p. 391

precipitación Agua que cae del aire a la superficie de la Tierra.

predator (PRED•uh•ter) An animal that hunts, catches, and eats other animals. p. 208

depredador Animal que caza, atrapa y come otros animales.

prey (PRAY) Animals that are caught and eaten by predators. p. 208

presa Animales que son atrapados y comidos por los depredadores.

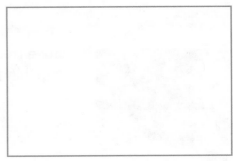

producer (pruh•DOOS•er) A living thing, such as a plant, that can make its own food. p. 182

productor Ser vivo, como las plantas, que es capaz de producir su propio alimento.

R

recycle (ree•sy•kuhl) To use the materials in old things to make new things. p. 470

reciclar Utilizar los materiales de cosas viejas para crear cosas nuevas.

reduce (ree•DOOS) To use less of something. p. 472

reducir Disminuir el uso de algo.

reuse (ree•YOOS) To use something again. p. 473

reutilizar Volver a usar algo.

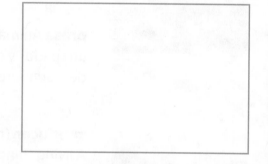

revolution (rev•uh•LOO•shuhn) The movement of Earth one time around the sun. p. 314

revolución Movimiento de la Tierra a lo largo de una órbita completa alrededor del Sol.

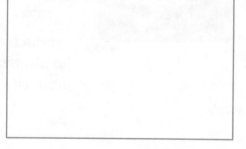

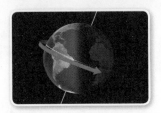

rotation (ro•TAY•shuhn) The turning of Earth on its axis. p. 297

rotación Giro de la Tierra sobre su propio eje.

S

scavenger (SKAV•in•jer) An animal that feeds on dead plants and animals. p. 227

carroñero Animal que se alimenta de plantas y animales muertos.

solution (suh•LOO•shuhn) A mixture that has the same composition throughout because all its parts are mixed evenly. p. 116

solución Mezcla que mantiene la misma composición a través de ella porque todas sus partes se han mezclado uniformemente.

S

system (SIS•tuhm) A set of connected things forming a complex whole. p. 368

sistema Conjunto de cosas conectadas entre sí que forman un todo complejo.

T

tradeoff (TRAID•awf) The process of giving up one quality or feature of a design to gain a different quality or feature.

intercambio Proceso de abandonar una cualidad o característica de un diseño para obtener una cualidad o característica diferente.

W

water cycle (WAW•ter SY•kuhl) The process in which water continuously moves from Earth's surface into the atmosphere and back again. p. 390

ciclo del agua Proceso en el que el agua se mueve continuamente desde la superficie terrestre hasta la atmósfera y de regreso.

Index

electricity, 110–111, 121, 139, 481–482

electroplating, 139

elevation, sight distance and, 278

El Niño, 426–427, 428

energy
    animal needs for, 180–181, 188, 236–238, 382
    conserving, 481–482, 484
    in ecosystems, 224–226, 235, 236–238
    in energy–matter cycle, 189, 236–238, 382
    energy pyramid, 236–238
    in photosynthesis, 170, 172, 182, 189, 382
    from renewable sources, 480
    solar power, 468, 480, 485
    from the sun, 182, 189, 295, 315, 396
    thermal, 391, 424–425
    in the water cycle, 391, 398

energy–matter cycle, 189, 236–238, 382

energy pyramid, 236–238

engineering
    definition, 6
    math in, 19–20
    models used in, 13
    parachute design, 287–288
    park path design, 29–33
    pollution cleanup device design, 199
    scientific discoveries used in, 11–12, 14
    U.S. Army Corps of Engineers, 259–260
    vision improvement, 11

engineering design process
    background research, 30–31, 33
    brainstorming, 32–33, 199
    collaborating and communicating, 39

criteria and constraints in, 28–29, 40
    defining a problem, 28–33
    in the Green Belt Movement, 42
    steps in design process, 38, 40
    testing design ideas, 38
    testing with a scale model, 34–37

Engineer It!
    carbon fiber, 83
    cleaning up pollution, 199
    gravity challenges, 286
    keeping track of time, 301
    observing objects in the sky, 320–321
    oil spill cleanup, 450
    plant watering system, 164
    reusing at home, 474
    space exploration computer models, 22
    space junk, 454
    toad trap, 254
    water quality, 428

engineers, 21–22, 60–62, 63–64

environment. See also ecosystems
    community, 205–206, 381
    definition, 198
    ecosystem, 198, 381
    forest, 198
    habitat, 198, 200–201, 406, 429–431
    niche, 200–201
    populations, 202–204, 205–206, 248, 381, 452

environmental protection
    conserving at home, 481–482
    green cities, 484–485
    green technology, 480, 484–485
    paper or plastic bag debate, 483
    pocket park, 486–490

recycling, 470–471, 475–478, 485
    reducing waste, 472
    reusing materials, 473, 475
    solar power, 468
    "three Rs," 470–473

Environmental Protection Agency (EPA), 61

erosion
    coastal, 420–423
    definition, 30, 400
    deforestation and, 41–42
    engineering controls on, 30–31
    from glaciers, 401
    of rock, 372
    from wind, 400

estuaries, 423

European Space Agency (ESA), 321

evaporation, 112–113, 164, 390–391, 398, 399

evidence
    in Evidence Notebook, for example, 10, 14, 27, 31, 33
    in Hands-On Activity, for example, 59, 135, 169, 187
    in Lesson Check, for example, 23, 43, 97, 123, 149
    in many lessons, for example, 6, 12, 13, 33, 51

Evidence Notebook
    Multiple assignments are given in every lesson. Example references are shown below, 55, 62, 65, 77, 79

exosphere, 373

explanation
    in every lesson, for example, 32, 39, 49, 60, 62, 131
    in Can You Explain It?, for example, 339, 367, 389, 413, 447